Is Everyone Hanging Out Without Me?

(And Other Concerns)

Is Everyone Hanging Out Without Me?
(And Other Concerns)

Mindy Kaling

CROWN
ARCHETYPE
NEW YORK

Published in the United States by Crown Archetype, an imprint of the
Crown Publishing Group, a division of Random House, Inc., New York.
www.crownpublishing.com

CROWN ARCHETYPE with colophon is a trademark of Random House, Inc.

Library of Congress Cataloging-in-Publication Data
Kaling, Mindy.
Is everyone hanging out without me? (and other concerns) /
Mindy Kaling. —1st ed.
p. cm.
1. American wit and humor. 2. Kaling, Mindy. I. Title.
PN6165.K35I8 2011
818'.602—dc23
2011033922

ISBN 978-0-307-88626-2
eISBN 978-0-307-88628-6

PRINTED IN THE UNITED STATES OF AMERICA

Book design by Elizabeth Rendfleisch
Jacket design by Laura Duffy
Jacket photography by Autumn de Wilde

Page 51, photo of Mindy Kaling and Conan O'Brien,
copyright © NBCU Photo Bank/Margaret Norton.
Page 113, photo of Mindy Kaling and Paul Lieberstein,
copyright © Michael Gallenberg.
Page 121, photo of Mindy Kaling directing Will Ferrell,
copyright © NBCU Photo Bank/Chris Haston/NBC.
All other photographs, *Matt & Ben* postcard,
and *Matt & Ben* script excerpt are courtesy of the author.

3   5   7   9   10   8   6   4   2

First Edition

For my parents

Contents

Is Everyone Hanging Out Without Me?

(And Other Concerns)

Hello

Introduction

THANK YOU for buying this book. Or, if my publisher's research analytics are correct, thank you, Aunts of America,
for buying this for your niece you don't know that well but really want to connect with more. There are many teenage vampire
books you could have purchased instead. I'm grateful you made
this choice.

I thought I'd take a minute to answer some questions:

What is this book about?
In this book I write a lot about romance, female friendships, unfair situations that now seem funny in retrospect, unfair situations that I still don't think are funny, Hollywood, heartache,
and my childhood. Just that really hard-core, masculine stuff
men love to read about. I wrote this book in a way that reflects
how I think. Sometimes it's an essay or story, and sometimes
it's a *pliest,* which is a piece with a list-y quality, a term I've just
made up.

Is this one of those guide books celebrities write for girls?
Oh, hell no. I'm only marginally qualified to be giving advice
at all. My body mass index is certainly not ideal, I frequently
use my debit card to buy things that cost less than three dollars,

because I never have cash on me, and my bedroom is so untidy it looks like vandals ransacked the Anthropologie Sale section. I'm kind of a mess. I did, however, fulfill a childhood dream of writing and acting in television and movies. Armed with that confidence, alongside a lifelong love of the sound of my own voice, yes, I've put some advice in this book.

However, you should know I disagree with a lot of traditional advice. For instance, they say the best revenge is living well. I say it's acid in the face—who will love them now? Another old saying is that revenge is a dish best served cold. But it *feels* best served piping hot, straight out of the oven of outrage. My opinion? Take care of revenge right away. Push, shove, scratch that person while they're still within arm's reach. Don't let them get away! Who knows when you'll get this opportunity again?

Do you offer up a lot of opinions in this book?
A little bit. I do lay in some opinions here and there. For example, I don't think it should be socially acceptable for people to say they are "bad with names." No one is bad with names. That is not a real thing. Not knowing people's names isn't a neurological condition; it's a choice. You *choose* not to make learning people's names a priority. It's like saying, "Hey, a disclaimer about me: I'm rude." For heaven's sake, if you don't know someone's name, just pretend you do. Do that thing everyone else does, where you vaguely say, "Nice to see you!" and make weak eye contact.

So, is this book like a women's magazine?
Not really, but if it reads like a really funny magazine, I'll be psyched. I love magazines. You can't walk by a magazine and not sit down and read it. You try to throw away a magazine and if you don't push it down in the trash enough, it somehow resurfaces on the floor of your TV room. I know this because I swear

my house has been haunted by the same December 2004 issue of *Glamour* magazine for the past seven years.

I'm buying this book for my daughter, whom I'm trying to reconnect with after my acrimonious divorce from her mother. Will this help me seem like a cool, understanding dad?
Honestly, I think you should buy her some kind of SUV. This is what all the divorced dads did for their kids in my high school. A Land Rover, something like that. If you don't have that kind of money, I would just suggest reconciling with the mom.

I don't know. I have a lot of books already. I wanted to finish those **Girl with the Dragon Tattoo** *books before the movies come out.*
This book will take you two days to read. Did you even see the cover? It's mostly pink. If you're reading this book every night for months, something is not right.

This sounds okay, but not as good as Tina Fey's book. Why isn't this more like Tina Fey's book?
I know, man. Tina's awesome. I think she may have every major international trophy for excellence except a Heisman. (She might actually have an honorary Heisman, I should check.) Unfortunately, I can't be Tina, because it's very difficult to lure her into a *Freaky Friday*-type situation where we could switch bodies, even though in the movies they make it look so easy. Believe me, I've tried.

What else should I know?
(1) There is no sunrise so beautiful that it is worth waking me up to see it.
(2) I would like to be friends with Beyoncé Knowles.

. . .

Well, I think I've covered everything and have still maintained an air of sexy mystery about myself. I feel good about
this.

Love,
Mindy

Alternate Titles for This Book

HERE WERE some titles for my book that I really liked but was advised strongly not to use.

The Girl with No Tattoo

When Your Boyfriend Fits into Your Jeans and Other Atrocities

The Book That Was Never a Blog

Always Wear Flats and Have Your Friends Sleep Over: A Step-by-Step How-To Guide for Avoiding Getting Murdered

Harry Potter Secret Book #8

Sometimes You Just Have to Put on Lip Gloss and Pretend to Be Psyched

I Want Dirk Nowitzki to Host *Saturday Night Live* So Much That I'm Making It the Title of My Book

Barf Me to Death and Other Things I've Been Known to Say

The Last Mango in Paris *(this would work best if "Mango" were the cheeky nickname for an Indian woman, and if I'd spent any time in Paris)*

So You've Just Finished Chelsea Handler's Book, Now What?

Deep-Dish Pizza in Kabul *(a touching novel about a brave girl enjoying Chicago-style pizza in secret Taliban-ruled Afghanistan)*

There Has Ceased to Be a Difference Between My Awake Clothes and My Asleep Clothes

I Don't Know How She Does It, But I Suspect She Gets Help from Illegal Immigrants

I Forget Nothing:
A Sensitive Kid
Looks Back

Chubby for Life

I DON'T REMEMBER a time when I wasn't chubby. Like being Indian, being chubby feels like it is just part of my permanent deal. I remember being in first grade, in Mrs. Gilmore's class at Fiske Elementary School, and seeing that Ashley Kemp, the most popular girl in our class, weighed only thirty-seven pounds. We knew this because we weighed her on the industrial postal scale they kept in the teacher's supply closet. I was so envious. I snuck into the supply closet later that same day to weigh myself. I was a whopping sixty-eight pounds.

Some of the first math I understood was that I was closer to twice Ashley's weight than to her weight.

"Don't be closer to *twice* a friend's weight than to her actual weight," I told myself. This little mantra has helped me stave off obesity for more than two decades.

My mom's a doctor, but because she came from India and then Africa, where childhood obesity was not a problem, she put no premium on having skinny kids. In fact, she and my dad didn't mind having a chubby daughter. Part of me wonders if it even made them feel a little prosperous, like *Have you seen our overweight Indian child? Do you know how statistically rare this is?* It will then not come as a surprise to you that I've never been thin in my life—except the day I was born, when I was six pounds.

It's a small point of pride that I was a six-pound baby, because from my limited understanding of baby weights, that's on the skinnier side. I flaunt my low baby weight the way really obese people must flaunt their dainty, small feet. It's my sole claim to skinny fame.

My older brother Vijay, and me, interrupted as I was plotting to eat him.

As you can see, from then on, however, it was full-speed-ahead food paradise! In grade school, I would vacillate along the spectrum from chubby to full-on fat until I was about fourteen. Being overweight is so common in America and comes in so many forms that you can't just call someone "fat" and have the reasonable expectation anyone will understand you. Here's the breakdown:

Chubby: A regular-size person who could lose a few, for whom you feel affection.

Chubster: An overweight, adorable child. That kid from *Two and a Half Men* for the first couple of years.

Fatso: An antiquated term, really. In the 1970s, mean sorority girls would call a pledge this. Probably most often used on people who aren't even really fat, but who fear being fat.

Fatass: Not usually used to describe weight, actually. This deceptive term is more a reflection of one's laziness. In the writers' room of *The Office,* an upper-level writer might get impatient and yell, "Eric, take your fat ass and those six fatasses and go write this B-story! I don't want to hear any more excuses why the plot doesn't make sense!"

Jabba the Hutt: *Star Wars* villain. Also, something you can call yourself after a particularly filling Thanksgiving dinner that your aunts and uncles will all laugh really hard at.

Obese: A serious, nonpejorative way to describe someone who is unhealthily overweight.

Obeseotron: A nickname you give to someone you adore who has just stepped on your foot accidentally, and it hurts. Alternatively, a fat robot.

Overweight: When someone is roughly thirty pounds too heavy for his or her frame.

Pudgy: See "Chubby."

Pudgo: See "Chubster."

Tub o' Lard: A huge compliment given by Depression-era people to other, less skinny people.

Whale: A really, really mean way that teen boys target teen girls. See the following anecdote.

DUANTE DIALLO

There have been two times in my life—ages fourteen and nineteen—when I lost a ton of weight over a short period of time. At fourteen, I lost the weight because of Duante Diallo.

In ninth grade, my class was made up mostly of the same kids with whom I had gone to middle school, with the exception of about twenty splashy new students. One of those students was Duante.

Duante Diallo was a handsome kid from Senegal who'd moved to Boston to play basketball for our school. He was immediately the star forward of our varsity basketball team. We had a not-great artsy-private-school basketball team, the kind made up of slender boys whose primary goal was to seem well-rounded for college applications. But you could tell Duante would've been the star of even a really good team. He was beloved by teachers because he was a brave kid for being so far away from his parents, and beloved by students because he was good-looking, a jock, and had an interesting African accent. Also, people couldn't believe the stuff he had done in Senegal, like smoke, drive a car, have sex, live in a village, and hold a gun. When he was introduced at a student assembly, he chose to give a short speech where he taught us a sports cheer in Senegalese. In the hallways, small crowds would form around Duante as he shared stories from his past. Once he shot a cow with an AK-47. He was so popular you could barely look at him without being blinded by cool.

Duante was also, unfortunately, a tyrannical asshole. Maybe I should have gleaned this from the joy with which he told the story about murdering a cow with a massive gun. He fixated on me early in the year as being overweight and was open with his observations. At first it had the veneer of niceness. For example, once I was getting a drink of water in the hallway where he and his friends were standing.

DUANTE: You would actually be really pretty if you lost weight.

His face was gentle and earnest, as though what he had really said was, "You remind me of a sunset in my native Senegal." It was confusing. All I could muster as a reply to this insulting comment was "thank you." I was hurt, but I rationalized that maybe Duante had been around only extremely thin African girls his whole third-world life and didn't know American girls had access to refrigeration, and that we didn't have to divide up UN food parcels with our neighbors. (This may have been a tad racist an assumption on my part. Look, we were both in the wrong.)

By winter, I had not lost any weight, and in fact had gained about ten more pounds. This really bothered Duante. I think he felt he had gone out of his way to give me some valuable advice and I had chosen not to follow it, therefore insulting him. One day in February, I walked into the freshmen center, he stopped mid-conversation with his friends and gestured to me.

DUANTE: Speaking of whales . . .

I don't even think they'd been talking about whales. The guys all laughed, but even I could tell some felt guilty doing it. I had been friends with most of them since we were kids. Danny Feinstein, who was my Latin study buddy, came up to me later that afternoon and told me that "What Duante said wasn't cool." He had a stoic look of noble do-gooder, although he had said nothing at the time of the insult. Again, I was forced to say thank you. How I continually found myself in situations where I felt I had to say thank you to mean guys, I'm not sure.

It was a tough winter. I had gone from competitive, bookish nerd to nervous target. If this was *Heathers,* I was Martha Dumptruck and this mean African kid was all three Heathers. I turned my obsessive teenage energy away from reading *Mad* magazine and focused on my diet. I didn't have access to a lot of weight-loss resources, because this was pre-Internet. There was one Weight Watchers near us, but it shared a mini-mall parking lot with a sketchy Salvation Army, and my parents didn't like the idea of taking me there for meetings. So I invented a makeshift diet formula: I would eat exactly half of what was put in front of me, and no dessert. Without exercising, I lost thirty pounds in about two months. A janitor at school whom I liked, Mrs. Carrington, would see me and say, "Damn, you've got a metabolism on you, don't you girl?" The janitors were always in my corner.

I remember waking up in the morning and looking down at my fingers and seeing they had shrunk overnight. Suddenly I was freezing all the time, like those skinny girls in movie theaters are always complaining about, and needed to sleep with an extra wool blanket. My face thinned out, and my belly went away. I stopped wearing oversize college sweatshirts and corduroy pants with elastic waists. Light brown lines appeared on my upper inner arms that looked like little rivers headed to my shoulder blades. I actually thought they looked pretty, until my mom told me they were stretch marks from losing so much weight so fast. It was like a Disney sci-fi movie. Mom was impressed but didn't want me to go overboard, which was impossible, because I was still eating a lot. I just had taken a break from eating like a professional football player. I loved all the side effects of losing the weight, but the reason I did it was so that Duante would stop making fun of me, so I could hang out in the freshmen center again, and not where I had been: across the street in the Fairy Woods.*

I thought Duante would finally leave me alone, but he didn't. One day I was walking down the hallway to class and passed Duante and his group of friends.

DUANTE: Remember when Mindy was like (blowing out his cheeks to make a fat face) a whale?

They all laughed. Come on, dude. *Remember when?* I'm getting made fun of because I *used* to be fat? The laws of bullying allow you to be cruel even when the victim had made strides for improvement? This is when I realized that bullies have no code of conduct.

Lucky for me, Duante was a bad student. English was his second language and that made everything harder for him. I delighted in the fact that he had to go to the middle school to take some of his classes. Sophomore year he broke his leg when he slipped during practice and collided with another student. For a short time he was even more popular, as sports injuries tend to make people, but then soon enough his crutches were tedious to people when he was slow-moving and hard to get around in the hallway. He didn't play that season, and was never as good at basketball after the injury. He dropped out junior year, and I heard he got a girl pregnant. Part of me now feels a little bad for Duante Diallo, but not at the time. I was so happy. That fucking mean Senegalese kid.

---

* The Fairy Woods was a small foresty area by the Charles River. This was where bad kids and frustrated teachers went to smoke. It was rumored to be a place where gay men had anonymous sex. This is why it had maturely been dubbed the Fairy Woods. I did not put this together until I was twenty-five.

AN INTERVENTION

I stayed at a pretty normal weight until college, when I put on the freshman thirty-five in the first six months. What's that? You've never heard of the freshman thirty-five? That's funny, because neither had my parents, who welcomed me home on spring vacation with mild horror. I was a vaguely familiar food monster who had eaten their daughter.

When I lost weight at nineteen, it was significant because that is when I first started exercising. I had always successfully avoided exercise as a kid, by being an extra in school plays, or signing up for fake-y sports like Tai Chi, or manipulating gym teachers into letting me read books in the bleachers. So it was at Dartmouth College, in 1999, that I discovered exercise when my best friend, Brenda, taught me how to run. I was a sloth upon whom Brenda took pity, and she saved me from near-obesity with the patience and tenacity of Annie Sullivan, the Miracle Worker.

Our workout routine was simple and mind-numbingly repetitive, an atmosphere in which I flourished, oddly. I started out walking for twenty minutes, and then Bren would make me do little spurts of running between lampposts or street signs. (For the record, Bren, a natural athlete, runs, like, a six-minute mile. This was an absolute waste of time for her. She was just doing this out of her well-brought-up Catholic kindness.) Then we'd come back to our apartment and do *Abs of Steel* together. Even though we mercilessly made fun of the video, which was from the deep eighties and included Tamilee Webb wearing aqua bike shorts and a pink thong leotard, we did it religiously. Tamilee had a rock-hard butt, and there was nothing ironic about it. The whole experience was surprisingly fun and cemented a friendship between Brenda and me for life. How can you not make a best friend out of a girl who has seen the sweat-soaked pelvis area of your gym pants, daily, and who still chooses to spend time with you? In this safe and friendly setting, I lost thirty pounds in a semester.

I LOVE DIETS

I wish I could just be one of those French women you read about who stays thin by eating only the most gourmet foods in tiny, ascetic proportions, but I could never do that. First of all, I largely don't *like* gourmet food. I *like* frozen yogurt. I think it tastes better than ice cream. I love diet soda; when I drink juice or regular soda it makes my blood sugar spike and I act like a cracked out Rachael Ray, but without the helpful household tips. I even like margarine, though everyone tells me it's basically poison or whatever. So, that's one thing I have going against me. Another obstacle is that my pattern is to eat exactly as much as whoever is hanging out with me, and between boyfriends and my tall athletic friends, we're a bunch of huge eaters. I really do have a remarkable appetite. I remember when the news reports came out about Michael Phelps's ten-thousand-calorie-a-day diet, and everyone was so shocked. But I just thought, *yep, I could do that, no problem.*

Ultimately, the main reasons why I will be chubby for life are (1) I have virtually no hobbies except dieting. I can't speak any non-English languages, knit, ski, scrapbook, or cook. I have no pets. I don't know how to do drugs. I lost my passport three years ago when I moved into my house and never got it renewed.

Video games scare me because they all seem to simulate situations I'd hate to be in, like war or stealing cars. So if I ever lost weight I would also lose my only hobby; (2) I have no discipline; I'm like if Private Benjamin had never toughened up but, in fact, got worse; (3) Guys I've dated have been into me the way I am; and (4) I'm pretty happy with the way I look, so long as I don't break a beach chair.

My love for dieting is a recent realization. It turns out I have a passion for trying out new eating plans and exercises. Dukan, South Beach, French Women Don't Get Fat, Cavemen Don't Get Fat, Single-Celled Organisms Don't Get Fat, Skinny Bitch, Skinny Wretch—after a while on one regimen, I get bored and want to try a new one. It's actually fun for me to read all the material and testimonials of the tan, shammy doctors who stand by the diets medically. It's only a matter of time before the Jane Austen Diet comes out, and I'm really looking forward to spending a spring adhering to that one.

If someone called me chubby, it would no longer be something that kept me up late at night. Duante Diallo has no power over me anymore, unless he was deported and he's grown up to be an African warlord or something and has a machete. Being called fat is not like being called stupid or unfunny, which is the worst thing you could ever say to me. Do I envy Jennifer Hudson for being able to lose all that weight and look smokin' hot? Of course, yes. Do I sometimes look at Gisele Bündchen and wonder how awesome life would be if I never had to wear Spanx? Duh, of course. That's kind of the point of Gisele Bündchen. I wish I could be like that, and maybe I will, once or twice, for a very short period of time. But on the list of things I want to do in my lifetime, that's not near the top. I mean, it's not near the bottom, either. I'd say it's right above "Learn to drive a Vespa," but several notches below "Film a chase scene for a movie."

I Am Not an Athlete

I KNOW, I KNOW. Did you put down this book in surprise? I've always been *extremely* bad at anything athletic. I know it sounds like hyperbole here, but this isn't like when I exclaim "I love that dress so much I want to kill myself." This is for real.

The strange thing is, I love watching certain sports as much as I detest participating in them myself. In the early 1980s, when my family was fixated on the Celtics-Lakers rivalry, I sat in front of the TV with them, thinking Larry Bird was the handsomest man in the world.* But if handed an actual basketball, I would instantly begin to cry. For me, doing sports was like meeting the Disney characters at Disney World. On TV I loved Mickey Mouse, but when I met the actual real-life Mickey, or rather, his impersonator, and he tried to hug me in his warm, fuzzy suit, I recoiled in fear.

PART ONE: BIKES

I learned to ride a bike at age twelve. That was crazy old for my neighborhood. I had been successfully avoiding learning for

---

* At the age of six, the criteria for handsome was, simply: "Is he not related to me?" and "Have I seen him on television?" That was it. By this standard, Larry Bird, Dick Clark, Andy Rooney. All handsome guys.

years, mostly by making a big show that I couldn't be torn away from whatever book I was reading. If my parents have any soft spot, it is for books, and I knew that the best way to get out of chores, or sports, or talking to elderly relatives on the phone was by holding up a book and saying, "But I'm just enjoying *Little House on the Prairie* so much!" I may have read the entire Laura Ingalls Wilder canon simply to get out of raking the lawn with my brother. But when other girls in my grade were starting to get their periods and I still didn't know how to ride a bike, the jig was glaringly up.

My dad finally had to get serious about this. Maybe he was worried I would go through life not participating in one of the Great American pastimes. Maybe he thought I had the potential to become a great cyclist. Or maybe he thought riding a bike would be a great way to flee assailants. Presumably he just wanted me to fit in with the kids who biked around, and to make some friends, and not be that strange girl who stayed in every weekend watching *The Golden Girls* with her mom.

Fueling my fight against my dad's wishes was my enormous dislike of bikes. Bikes were horrible. Bikes always seemed to be scratching against my legs, or the spoke was poking me or something. Pebbles ended up in my ankle socks when I was on a bike. The seat felt sharp and hurt my crotch. The bike represented everything annoying and uncomfortable in my young life.

Wearing elbow pads, knee pads, and a helmet, I took my bike to the parking lot behind the Beth Shalom synagogue across the street. Dad came with me, holding two huge bottles of Gatorade. I was obsessed with not getting dehydrated while learning to ride a bike. It took me a week to find my balance, because once I took both feet off the ground, I employed the ace move of closing my eyes out of fear.

"What are you doing? Open your eyes!" my dad shouted.

So, it turns out that keeping your eyes open is the key to

learning to ride a bike. Once I mastered balance, my dad left me alone to do bike drills so I'd have it ingrained. "Doing drills until it's ingrained" is actually a classic Indian technique of teaching children things that goes back to Sanskrit liturgical texts. Index cards and Sharpie pens are actually distinctly Indian cultural artifacts to me. I rode my bike, for hours, around the parking lot behind Beth Shalom. Let me remind you that this was before iPods. This was even before those bright yellow sports Walkmans. With no music to listen to, I just biked around in circles talking to myself like a kid on the cover of a Robert Cormier young adult novel, circling around puzzled Jewish families walking back to their cars. This is how I learned to ride a bike.

What my dad didn't realize at the time was that while I was cementing the mechanics of riding the bike, I was also cementing my hatred for doing it. I just decided I hated it, and that was that. You cannot begin to understand the power of my irrational hatred at twelve years old, but it's the kind of hatred that lasts. It was the same mysterious and powerful hatred that reared its head later in life for other things, like hiking, orientation games, and having to watch any kind of pageant whatsoever.

PART TWO: FRISBEE

Even though I wisely chose a group of friends who weren't too athletic, the Frisbee has been a recurring nuisance in my life. Frisbee, or "disc," as I have been corrected angrily many times, is one of the few sports artsy kids like to do, and so we've inevitably crossed paths. A good thing to know about me is that I'm terrible at Frisbee and I hate playing it so much. Catching it, obviously (I mean, close your eyes. Can you seriously picture me catching a Frisbee? No! You can't even picture it *in your imagination*) but throwing as well. It always goes down like this: my

Frisbee enthusiast friends insist that I would love Frisbee if I were taught how to throw. I decline. They persist, and I relent. So after careful instruction by my friends—but really, who has ever been able to make use of the advice "it's all in the wrist"?—I give it a shot. I hurl the Frisbee (at some crazy-fast speed and far distance; I have always had meaty, strong arms) in completely the wrong direction until it lands on the other side of the park.

Unlike other athletes, Frisbee people won't let it go. My theory is that this is because there's a huge overlap between people who are good at Frisbee and people who do Teach for America. The same instinct to make at-risk kids learn, which I admire so much, becomes deadly when turned on friends trying to relax on a Sunday afternoon in the park. They feel they have to corral me into learning this useless sport. The afternoon becomes "unlocking Mindy's passion for Frisbee," instead of letting me lie on the grass reading my chick lit book. How dare you? If I had thought learning Frisbee was a valuable thing to do, I would've done it. I don't want to learn! I don't want to learn! Let me read *Shopaholic Runs for Congress* in peace!

PART THREE: ROPES

There is a famous photo of my older brother, Vijay, my cousin Hondo, and me climbing ropes at the Josiah Willard Hayden Recreation Centre in Lexington, Massachusetts, in 1984, when we were seven, six, and five years old, respectively. Famous in the sense that the local newspaper, *The TAB,* ran the picture for some reason. I guess the sight of three little Indian kids in roughly identical outfits with roughly the same haircut climbing ropes was interesting to their readers. But I remember, even as a five-year-old, thinking, *Why am I being made to do this? I never see Mom and Dad climbing ropes! You can't tell me this is useful!*

What the photo didn't show was that after it was taken,

I climbed all the way up, which took me about forty minutes. Once at the top, I didn't like the view and refused to climb down. Also my thighs were badly chafed and I had to go to the bathroom. Eventually, my counselors had to hoist up a ladder and pull me down, much to the embarrassment of Vijay and Hondo. I'm pretty sure Vijay claimed that Hondo was his sibling and I was the cousin.

Luckily the rope fiasco was eclipsed, several weeks later, when I accidentally pronounced *jalapeño* with a hard *j* in front of Vijay, Hondo, and some other campers. I'd only ever seen it printed on the side of a can of salsa. "You think it's *ja-lapeno*?!" Hondo asked, incredulous. I did.

Vijay, Hondo, and me in descending order.

PART FOUR: MORSES POND

Amazingly, there is actually another instance from my childhood where I froze in the middle of an athletic pursuit, and it was much more serious. It occurred at Wellesley Summer Day Camp, where my brother and I were shipped out to as kids in the '80s. The camp made daily visits to Morses Pond in Wellesley, Massachusetts. I didn't like Morses Pond because there was no snack bar or gift shop like at Walden Pond. Where it had a significant leg up over Walden was that at least it didn't have a scary ghost haunting it, which is who I assumed Henry David Thoreau was, and why everyone made such a big deal about him. A few years after I swam there as a kid, they made Morses Pond off-limits to swimmers. Apparently, it was saturated with contaminated soil from an abandoned paint factory. To its credit, I only remember it teeming with Canadian geese poop. Then, a few years after it was condemned, a rich physician hired a hit man to murder his wife there. This really happened. I know what you're thinking. Morses Pond? More like *Remorses Pond*! But now it's open again.

I took this photo one busy summer afternoon.
Note: if you want to seem like a super-creepy person, be an adult,
by yourself, taking photos of children and people on a beach.

As a kid, I was curious but not remotely adventurous, if that makes sense. I wanted to climb the diving board to see the view out to the other side of Morses Pond, but I didn't want to swim over there. The far side of the pond was so filled with weeds and algae that it was a pretty copper-y color, and I wanted to get a better view. Once I got to the top of the ladder to the diving board, I could see way across the pond. The weeds and algae were indeed very pretty. Even further out, I saw Wellesley Center, where my favorite children's bookstore was. I was glad I did it, and I turned to climb down.

That's when Scott, the handsome counselor who was wading in the deep end of the pond, yelled up at me. (Again, not sure if he was actually handsome, or just handsome by my aforementioned criteria.)

SCOTT: You're not allowed to climb back down the ladder! You have to dive!

I froze. This was the big-kid diving board and it really was extremely high. I inched backward, pretending not to hear.

SCOTT: Don't even think about it. It's against the rules. Once you're up there, there's only one way down.

ME: Is that the camp's rules or the pond's rules?

There was a pause as Scott thought about this. It annoyed him that I had a follow-up question.

SCOTT: It's the same. You *cannot* climb back down!

ME: I really don't want to jump.

SCOTT: Well, you're just going to stand there, then.

Two bigger kids were now standing at the base of the ladder, impatiently waiting for their turn.

I think it was the most scared I've ever been in my life. I was too scared to jump off, but I was also scared of getting in trouble with the camp and of bringing shame to my family. And, most important, embarrassing Vijay. (Summers at this point were just a terrifying countdown to the moment when I would somehow embarrass my poor older brother, whose shame stung worse than my own. Would I eat too many Popsicles at lunch, leaving none for some other kid and leave myself open to ridicule as Popsicle Pig? Would I get a mud stain on the back of my shorts and become Shitty Pants?)

Scott probably thought he was doing something really good for me, or maybe this was something his mean stepdad did to him and he was exorcising the bad experience on me, but whatever he was trying to do, it sucked. All I remember is crazy, panicky, ice-cold fear shooting through my limbs. Unable to say, "Screw you, dude, I'm going down the ladder, and I'm going to call my mom from the payphone to pick me up and take me home," I closed my eyes and just let myself fall into the water.

The sight of a fat child falling, lifeless, from a high distance into a pond is kind of an amazing sight, I'll bet. You know when a kid's getting a shot or a tooth removed, how you tell them that it's not going to be as bad as they're imagining it will be? Well, this was a hundred times worse than what I had imagined.

First of all, it *hurt*. I don't know how it happened, but I got a huge cut from falling into the water. (It was on the back of my left knee; to this day, I have a four-inch dark brown scar there.) Three people, including Scott, pulled me out of the water. They rushed me to shore, to the First Aid room, which, weirdly, had injections for anaphylactic shock and an eye wash but no paper towels. Scott patted down the back of my leg with beach towels.

Ultimately they got it to stop bleeding, and Scott begged me not to tell my parents. I remember him asking me four or five times. God knows what that must've looked like to an observer, a seventeen-year-old boy exhorting a disoriented, bleed-

The scene of the cover-up.

ing six-year-old "not to tell her parents" something. But this was Morses Pond, and that's the kind of thing that happened there.

Lessons? When I was kid, my parents smartly raised us to keep quiet, be respectful to older people, and generally not question adults all that much. I think that's because they were assuming that 99 percent of time, we'd be interacting with worthy, smart adults, like my aunts and uncles; my teachers; my ancient and knowledgeable piano instructor, Mrs. Brewster; and police officers. They didn't ever tell me, "Sometimes you will meet idiots who are technically adults and authority figures. You don't have to do what they say. You can calmly say, 'Can I first call my mom and ask if I have to do this, please?' " But we didn't have cell phones back then. The only people with cell phones were rich villains in action movies you knew were going to die first.

When I have kids I will largely follow how my parents raised me, because, like everyone else on the planet, I think my parents are perfect and so am I. But one thing I will impart to my children is "If you're scared of something, that isn't a sign that you have to do it. It probably means you *shouldn't* do it. Call Dad or Mom immediately."

. . .

A handful of bad experiences when I was small have made me a confirmed nonathlete. In psychology (okay, *Twilight*) they teach you about the notion of imprinting, and I think it applies here. I reverse-imprinted with athleticism. Ours is the great non-love story of my life.

Don't Peak in High School

SOMETIMES TEENAGE girls ask me for advice about what they should be doing if they want a career like mine one day. There are basically two ways to get where I am: (1) learn a provocative dance and put it on YouTube; (2) convince your parents to move to Orlando and homeschool you until you get cast on a kids' show, *or* do what I did, which is (3) stay in school and be a respectful and hardworking wallflower, and go to an accredited non-online university.

Teenage girls, please don't worry about being super popular in high school, or being the best actress in high school, or the best athlete. Not only do people not care about any of that the second you graduate, but when you get older, if you reference your successes in high school too much, it actually makes you look kind of pitiful, like some babbling old Tennessee Williams character with nothing else going on in her current life. What I've noticed is that almost no one who was a big star in high school is also big star later in life. For us overlooked kids, it's so wonderfully *fair*.

I was never the lead in the play. I don't think I went to a single party with alcohol at it. No one offered me pot. It wasn't until I was sixteen that I even knew marijuana and pot were the same thing. I didn't even learn this from a cool friend; I gleaned it from a syndicated episode of *21 Jump Street*. My parents didn't let me do social things on weeknights because weeknights were for homework, and *maybe* an episode of *The X-Files* if I was being a good kid (*X-Files* was on Friday night), and *on extremely rare occasions* I could watch *Seinfeld* (Thursday, a school night), if I had just aced my PSATs or something.

It is easy to freak out as a sensitive teenager. I always felt I was missing out because of the way the high school experience was dramatized in television and song. For every realistic *My So-Called Life*, there were ten *90210*s or *Party of Five*s, where a twenty-something Luke Perry was supposed to be just a typical guy at your high school. If Luke Perry had gone to my high school, everybody would have thought, "What's the deal with this brooding greaser? Is he a narc?" But that's who Hollywood put forth as "just a dude at your high school."

In the genre of "making you feel like you're not having an awesome American high school experience," the worst offender is actually a song: John Cougar Mellencamp's "Jack and Diane." It's one of those songs—like Eric Clapton's "Tears in Heaven"— that everyone knows all the words to without ever having chosen to learn them. I've seen people get incredibly pumped when this song comes on; I once witnessed a couple request it four times in a row at Johnny Rockets and belt it while loudly clapping their hands above their heads, so apparently it is an anthem of some people's youth. I think across America, as I type this, there are high school couples who strive to be like Jack and Diane from that song. Just hangin' out after school, makin' out at the Tastee Freez, sneakin' beers into their cars, without a care in the world. Just two popular, idle, all-American white kids, having a blast.

The world created in "Jack and Diane" is maybe okay-charming because, like, all right, that kid Jack is going to get shipped off to Vietnam and there was going to be a whole part two of the story when he returned as some traumatized, disillusioned vet. The song is only interesting to me as the dreamy first act to a much more interesting *Born on the Fourth of July*–type story.

As it is, I guess I find "Jack and Diane" a little disgusting.

As a child of immigrant professionals, I can't help but notice the wasteful frivolity of it all. Why are these kids not home doing their homework? Why aren't they setting the table for dinner or helping out around the house? Who allows their kids to hang out in parking lots? Isn't that loitering?

I wish there was a song called "Nguyen and Ari," a little ditty about a hardworking Vietnamese girl who helps her parents with the franchised Holiday Inn they run, and does homework in the lobby, and Ari, a hardworking Jewish boy who does volunteer work at his grandmother's old-age home, and they meet after school at Princeton Review. They help each other study for the SATs and different AP courses, and then, after months of studying, and mountains of flashcards, they kiss chastely upon hearing the news that they both got into their top college choices. This is a song teens need to inadvertently memorize. Now that's a song I'd request at Johnny Rockets!

In high school, I had fun in my academic clubs, watching movies with my girlfriends, learning Latin, having long, protracted, unrequited crushes on older guys who didn't know me, and yes, hanging out with my family. I liked hanging out with my family! Later, when you're grown up, you realize you never get to hang out with your family. You pretty much have only eighteen years to spend with them full time, and that's it. So, yeah, it all added up to a happy, memorable time. Even though I was never a star.

Because I was largely overlooked at school, I watched everyone like an observant weirdo, not unlike Eugene Levy's character Dr. Allan Pearl in *Waiting for Guffman,* who "sat next to the class clown, and studied him." But I did that with everyone. It has helped me so much as a writer; you have no idea.

I just want ambitious teenagers to know it is totally fine to be quiet, observant kids. Besides being a delight to your parents, you will find you have plenty of time later to catch up. So many people I work with—famous actors, accomplished writers—were overlooked in high school. Be like Allan Pearl. Sit next to the class clown and study him. Then grow up, take everything you learned, and get paid to be a real-life clown, unlike whatever unexciting thing the actual high school class clown is doing now.

The chorus of "Jack and Diane" is: *Oh yeah, life goes on, long after the thrill of living is gone.*

Are you kidding me? The thrill of living was *high school*? Come on, Mr. Cougar Mellencamp. Get a life.

Is Everyone Hanging Out Without Me?
(Or, How I Made My First Real Friend)

IN NINTH GRADE I had a secret friend. Her name was Mavis Lehrman. Mavis lived a few streets away from me in a Tudor-style house that every Halloween her parents made look like the evil witch's cottage from *Hansel and Gretel*. (This is amazing, by the way. It behooves anyone who lives in a Tudor house to make it look like a witch cottage once in a while.) The Lehrmans were a creative and eccentric family who my parents deemed good people. Mavis was my Saturday friend, which meant she came over to my house Saturday and we spent the afternoon watching television together.

Mavis and I bonded over comedy. It didn't matter if it was good or bad; at fourteen, we didn't really know the difference. We were comedy nerds, and we just loved watching and talking about it nonstop. We holed up in my family's TV room with blankets and watched hours of Comedy Central. Keep in mind this is not the Comedy Central of today, with the abundance of great shows like *South Park, The Daily Show,* and *The Colbert Report*. This was the early '90s, where you had to really search around to find decent stuff to watch. We'd start with the good shows, *Dr. Katz, Kids in the Hall,* or *Saturday Night Live* reruns, but when those were over, we were lucky if there was some dated movie playing like *Porky's* or *Kentucky Fried Movie*. With all the raunchy '80s sex comedies Comedy Central played, at times it felt like we were watching a confusing soft-core porn channel. It wasn't our favorite programming, but like the tray of croissants from Costco my mom left for us on the kitchen table, Mavis and I devoured it nonetheless. We loved comedy and wanted to watch everything. And more than that, we loved reenacting what we saw. The Church Lady's catchphrases were our catchphrases, and we repeated them until my mother said, exasperated: "Please stop saying 'Isn't that special?' in that strange voice. It is annoying to me and to others."

At fourteen, Mavis was already five foot ten. She had short, dark, slicked-back hair like Don Johnson in *Miami Vice*. She was very skinny and had women's size eleven feet. I know this because she accidentally wore my dad's boat shoes home one time. Mavis was a big, appreciative eater, which my parents loved. When she visited, she made a habit of immediately opening the fridge and helping herself to a heaping bowl of whatever leftover Indian food we had and a large glass of orange juice. "This *roti* and *aloo gobi* is delicious, Dr. Chokalingam," she'd say to my mother, between bites. "You should start a restaurant." My mother always protested when Mavis called her by the formal "Dr." name, but I think it secretly pleased her. She was sick of some of my other friends saying things like: "Hey, Swati, how's the practice going?" in that modern, we-call-parents-by-their-first-names fashion of liberally raised East Coast kids. Both my parents were very fond of Mavis. Who wouldn't love a hungry, complimentary, respectful kid?

But that was Saturday. At school, I had a completely different set of friends.

My posse at school was tight, and there were exactly four of us: Jana, Lauren, Polly, and me. We had been friends since middle school, which was only two years, but seemed like a lifetime.

The number of people in our friend group was important because of all the personalized best friend gear we had that read "JLMP," the first letters of our first names. We had JLMP beaded bracelets, JLMP embroidered bobby socks. We commissioned a caricature artist at Faneuil Hall in Boston to do a cartoon of the four of us with JLMP in giant cursive letters underneath. These mementos cemented our foursome to both us and the other people at school. You couldn't get in, and you couldn't get out. Nothing says impenetrability and closeness like a silk-screened T-shirt with an acronym most people don't understand. JLMP knew who Mavis was—she was a lifer at our school, which meant she had been there since kindergarten, and longer than any of us had been there—but she made no impact on our view of the social landscape. We didn't really talk or think about her; it was as if she was a substitute Spanish teacher or something.

The Cheesecake Factory played a major role in JLMP's social life. We went there every Friday after school. These were our wild Friday night plans. Remember, this was back in the '90s, before the only way to be a cool teenager was to have a baby or a reality show (or both). We'd stay for hours chewing on straws and gossiping about boys, and collectively only spend about fifteen dollars on one slice of cheesecake and four Cokes. Then we'd leave and have our regular dinners at our respective homes. Obviously, the waiters loathed us. In a way we were worse than the dine-and-dashers because at least the dine-and-dashers only hit up Cheesecake Factory once and never showed up again. We, on the other hand, thought we were beloved regulars and that people lit up when we walked in. *We're back, Cheesecake Factory! JLMP's back! Your favorite cool, young people here to jazz up the joint!*

I know what you're thinking, that I ditched Mavis because she wasn't as cool as my more classically "girly" friends, but that wasn't it. First of all, JLMP wasn't even very cool. High school girls who have time to be super cliquey are usually not the popular girls. The actual popular girls have boyfriends, and, by that point, have chilled out on intense girl friendships to explore sex and stuff. Not us. Sex? Forget it. JLMP had given up on that happening until grad school. Yep, we were the kind of girls who, at age fourteen, pictured ourselves attending grad school. Getting a good idea of us now?

Mavis had her own friends. Maybe because of her height and short hair, she hung out with mostly guys. Her crowd was the techie boys, the ones who built the sets at school and proudly wore all black, covered in dried paint splatter. The techie boys all had fancy names like "Conrad" and "Xander" and "Sebastian." It's as if their parents had hoped that by naming them these manly, ornate names, they might have a fighting chance of being the leading men of our school. Unfortunately, the actual leading men in our school were named "Matt" or "Rob" or "Chris" and wouldn't be caught dead near our student theater unless they were receiving a soccer trophy in a sports assembly. Mavis and her guy pals built gorgeous sets for our plays like *Evita, Rags,* and *City of Angels,* and got absolutely zero recognition for it. They were just kind of expected to build the sets, like the janitors were expected to clean up the hallways.

Though Mavis could have been confused for a boy from almost every angle, she had the pale skin and high cheekbones of an Edith Wharton character. Thinking back on her now, she had all the prerequisites to be a runway model in New York, especially since this was the early '90s, when it was advantageous to look like a flat-chested, rail-thin boy. But our school was behind the times, and the aesthetic that ruled was the curvy, petite, all-American Tiffani Amber Thiessen look, which Polly and Lauren had to some degree. At school, Mavis was considered neither pretty nor popular. Neither was I, by any stretch of the imagination, but at least I didn't tower over the boys in our class by a good five inches.

We both lived by a weird code: Mavis and I might be friends on Saturday afternoon, but Friday nights and weekend sleepovers were for JLMP. If it sounds weird and compartmentalized, that's because it was. But I was used to compartmentalization. My entire teenage life was a highly organized map of activities: twenty minutes to shower and get ready for school, five-minute breakfast, forty-five-minute Latin class to thirty-minute lunch to forty-five-minute jazz band rehearsal, etc. Compartmentalizing friendships did not feel different to me. Mavis and I would say "hi" in the hallways, and we would nod at each other. Occasionally we would sit next to each other in study hall. But Mavis did not fit into my life as my school friend.

Then things started to change.

One Saturday night, I had JLMP over my house. They wanted to watch *Sleeping with the Enemy,* you know, the movie where Julia Roberts fakes her own death to avoid being married to her psycho husband? And I wanted to watch *Monty Python's Flying Circus* and show them the Ministry of Silly Walks, one of their funniest and most famous sketches. Mavis and I had watched it earlier that day several times in a row, trying to imitate the walks ourselves. I played it for them. No one laughed. Lauren said: "I don't get it." I played it again. Still no response to it. I couldn't believe it. The very same sketch that had made Mavis and me clutch our chests in diaphragm-hurting laughter had rendered my best friends bored and silent. I made the classic mistake of trying to explain why it was so funny, as though a great explanation would be the key to eliciting a huge laugh from them. Eventually Polly said, gently, "I guess it's funny in a random kind of way."

Within the hour we were watching Julia Roberts flushing her wedding ring down the toilet and starting a new life in Iowa under an assumed identity. I could barely enjoy the movie, still stunned by my closest friends' utter lack of interest in something I loved so much. I had always known, yeah, maybe JLMP wouldn't be as interested in comedy as Mavis had been, but it scared me that they dismissed it so completely. I felt like two different people.

What happened to me was something that I think happens to a lot of professional comedy writers or comedians, or really anyone who's passionate about anything and discovering it for the first time. Most people who do what I do are obsessed with comedy, especially during adolescence. I think we all have that moment when our non-comedy-obsessed friends or family are like: "Nope. I'm at my limit. I can't talk about *In Living Color* anymore. It's kind of funny, but come on."

And more and more, I found that I didn't want to do what JLMP wanted to do. Like one time Lauren wanted me go to the yarn store in Harvard Square with her so we could both learn to knit. I reluctantly used my allowance to buy a skein of yarn. Who was I knitting stuff for? If I gave my mother a knitted scarf she'd be worried I was wasting my time doing stupid stuff like knitting instead of school work. Presenting a homemade knitted object to my parents was actually like handing them a detailed backlog of my idleness.

And Jana, sweet old Jana, was crazy about horses. Like super-nutso crazy about horses—that was her thing. All her drawings and back-from-vacation stories and Halloween costumes were horses. She would even pretend to be a horse during free period and lunch. We had to feed her pizza out of our hand, and she'd neigh back "thank you." Now I was getting bored of driving forty-five minutes with her parents to the equestrian center to pretend to care about her galloping back and forth in her horse recital or whatever.

I found myself wanting to spend more time with Mavis than JLMP. I spent the week looking forward to Saturday so I could write sketches with her. I didn't want her to be my secret friend anymore.

One Friday in November I didn't go to the Cheesecake Factory with JLMP. I asked Mavis if she wanted to hang out at the mall after school. We had never spent time together outside of our houses. Mavis was surprised but agreed to go. We went to the Arsenal Mall after school. We bought sour gummy worms at the bulk candy store; we walked around Express and The Limited, trying things on and buying nothing. It felt weird being with Mavis in the real world, but good-weird.

The next Friday I bailed on JLMP again so my brother, Mavis, and I could see *Wayne's World* together. We spend the whole night afterward chanting: "Wayne's World! Party Time! Excellent! Schwing!" Mavis and I spent a long time discussing Rob Lowe's emergence as a comedy actor. (Again, we were comedy nerds. This was exciting to us.) The following Friday we went to her house where Mr. Lehrman showed us how to use his camcorder so we could tape a sketch we had written, which used the characters in Gap Girls, that old *SNL* sketch with Chris Farley, Adam Sandler, and David Spade dressed up as female Gap employees. Mavis played David Spade and Adam Sandler. I played Chris Farley and all the other characters. Sometime around then, Mavis and I became real friends. Friends at school.

I spent most of winter break with Mavis, going to Harvard Square to see movies and buying comic books. I discovered she wasn't into going shopping as much as JLMP had been, but I had my mom and Aunt Sreela for that, anyway. I still considered JLMP my best friends, but began flaking on them more and more. Jana's mom even called my mom to tell her how hurt Jana was that I missed a big horse show. One Friday evening in mid-February, Mavis and I were at the RadioShack trying to find a tripod to use with her dad's camcorder. It was the mall with JLMP's Cheesecake Factory. On the escalator ride down, you could see right into the restaurant. That's when Mavis and I saw it. Jana, Lauren, and Polly were sitting in a booth together.

They were laughing and talking over a slice of cheesecake, but without me. Just JLP. I was so hurt and embarrassed. Yeah, I had made another friend, but did that give them the right to orchestrate a hangout where I was so left out? For a second, I hated Mavis. I wasn't sure why, exactly, maybe for witnessing this humiliation, or for unwittingly being the cause of it? My immediate reaction was to rush over to them and confront them. But then I thought . . . why? What was I going to do with them after I confronted them? Sit with them and gossip about all the things I didn't really care about anymore?

Mavis said, quietly, "If you want to go with them, I totally get it."

There was something about the unexpectedly kind way she said that that made me happy to be with her, and not them. For some reason, I immediately thought about how my parents had always been especially fond of Mavis, and here was this moment when I understood exactly why: she was a good person. It felt so good to realize how smart my parents had been all along. "Are you kidding me?" I said. "We have to go home and film this sketch."

By the time we got down the escalator and walked to the parking lot to get picked up by her parents, my ego was still bruised, but I was also able to identify another feeling: relief.

Pretty soon after that, the rest of JLP disintegrated too. Polly was getting into music more and was getting chummier with the kids who all smoked regularly across the street in the Fairy Woods. It was Jana, surprisingly, who first got a boyfriend. A cool Thai kid named Prem, who was a senior, asked her out. Prem was pretty possessive, and within weeks Jana was learning Thai and I never saw her. Lauren and I, with whom I had the least in common, faded out quickly without the buffer of the other two. It was almost a lifting of a burden when we weren't required to stay in touch.

By the end of freshman year, it was just Mavis and me. I once half-jokingly suggested naming our friendship M&M, and Mavis looked at me with friendly but mild disgust. That was so not Mavis's style. She stayed friends with her techie guy friends, and I even had lunch with them sometimes. They were smart guys, funny and edgier than any other guys at school, and they were knowledgeable about politics, a subject barely anyone cared about. But my friend group definitely shrunk. I was without a posse, no small herd to confidently walk down the hall with. There was just Mavis and me, but it never seemed lonely because we never stopped talking. I could have an argument, in earnest, about who was the best "Kid" in the Hall, without having to explain who they were. One friend with whom you have a lot in common is better than three with whom you struggle to find things to talk about. We never needed best friend gear because I guess with real friends you don't have to make it official. It just is.

Junior year of high school, the Lehrmans moved to Evanston, Illinois, but Mavis and I kept in touch. She would call me and tell me about the amazing shows her dad took her to see at Second City, and we planned for me to visit, but it never materialized. When we graduated high school, she went to the Cooper Union in Manhattan to pursue her love of set design, and I went to Dartmouth to pursue my love of white people and North Face parkas. We e-mailed a bit for a year or so, and then by sophomore year, the e-mails stopped. We both just got so consumed with college. I would be reminded of Mavis when my parents asked about her over summer and holiday breaks. "How is Mavis doing these days?" my mom would ask. "I think pretty good," I replied, vaguely, reminding myself to send her an e-mail one of these days, but never following through.

Mavis helped me learn so much about who I am, and who I wanted to be. I love comedy and now surround myself with people who love to talk about it just as much as I do. I like to think that Polly is in a band, that Lauren joined the right knitting circle, and that Jana found a nice horse to settle down with. Even though Mavis was my secret friend, she is the only one I hope I see again. She's the only one I wonder about. I hope she wonders about me too.

I Love New York
and It Likes Me Okay

Failing at Everything
in the Greatest City on Earth

I WAS HESITANT to write this essay because, of course, I would rather you guys think I'm some kind of wide-eyed wunderkind who just kind of floated into my job at *The Office* without even trying. I want you to picture me as a cute little anime character that popped out from behind a mushroom or something and landed in Hollywood. But writing about my struggles was actually really fun. Besides, who wants to read about success, anyway? Successful serial murderers, maybe.

COLLEGE RUINED ME

Not to sound braggy or anything, but I kind of killed it in college. You know that saying "big fish in a small pond"? At Dartmouth College, I was freakin' Jaws in a community swimming pool. I wrote plays, I acted, I sang, I was the student newspaper cartoonist. All this, of course, was less a function of my talent than of the school's being in rural New Hampshire, where the only option for real entertainment was driving one and a half hours to Manchester, on the off chance the Capitol Steps were touring there.

After beer pong, floating in an inner tube down the Connecticut River, fraternity hazing rituals, building effigies and burning them down in the center of our quad, a cappella, and driving to Montreal for strip clubs, student-run theatrical productions placed a strong seventh in terms of what was fun to do on campus. We had a captive audience with low standards, which was a recipe for smashing success and the reason for the inflated sense of self I have to this very day. If you're a kid who was not especially a star in your high school, I recommend going to a college in the middle of nowhere. I got all the attention I could ever have wanted. If I had gone to NYU, right now I'd be the funniest paralegal in a law firm in Boston.

I got even more confidence from having a steadfast companion in my best friend, Brenda. A few words about Brenda. Bren is the shit. In college, she was the star of every play at Dartmouth from her freshman fall on. She looked the way a Manhattan socialite should look: perfect posture, gazelle-like, with a sheet of dark blond hair. Girls always worried she was going to steal their boyfriends, but she never did. (I didn't understand that at all. It's college! Steal some boyfriends, for God's sake!) Bren and I befriended each other early on, became inseparable through a shared sense of humor, a trove of nonsensical private jokes, and had the same enemies within the Drama Department. We clung to each other with blind loyalty, like Lord Voldemort and his snake, Nagini. I, of course, was Nagini. If you messed with one of us, you knew you messed with both of us, and Voldemort was going to cast a murder spell on you, or Nagini was going to chomp on your jugular. It was such a good, dramatic time. Bren was the kind of best friend I dreamed about having when I was a little kid. I never knew you could have someone in your life who was pretty much on the same page about essentially everything.

In theater, Bren would play Beatrice or Medea or Eliza Doolittle, while I wrote well-attended comedy one-acts and occasionally played Medea's little buddy or something. I felt like a big celebrity on campus. Well, the kind of celebrity you could

In 2010, Bren was my date to the Emmys. People thought
she was on *Mad Men* and I was her publicist.

conceivably be at Dartmouth if you weren't a jock or a sorority
girl, who were the real celebrities. My fame was akin to that of,
say, Camilla Parker Bowles.

Our other best friend, Jocelyn, whom we met through our
singing group, was more or less the one directly responsible for
making the traditional college experience really fun. She was
less competitive and intense, and from Hawaii, so she was very
comfortable being naked, which was new to us and intimidat-
ing. She, along with our other friend Christina, made us go berry
picking and get our faces painted for football games, and she'd
host dinners in our shared dorm dining room. Jocelyn is willowy

Jocelyn and Brenda being really adorable at something
I don't remember being invited to.

and half-Asian, and while fitting the bill technically for a model, has no interest in modeling. She's just that cool. Me, on the other hand, whenever I lose, like, five pounds, I basically start considering if I should "try out" modeling. When the three of us walked down the street together, I looked like the Indian girl who kept them "real." I don't care. After all these years with friends who are five ten or taller, I have come to carry myself with the confidence of a tall person. It's all in the head. It works out.

So I left college feeling like a successful, awesome, tall person. Then, in July of 2001, the three of us moved to New York.

LATE NIGHT DREAMS, QUICKLY EXTINGUISHED

The job I most wanted in the world was to be a writer on *Late Night with Conan O'Brien*. I can't believe that was two Conan shows ago. It seems like yesterday.

I'd been an intern at *Late Night* three years before and was famously one of the worst interns the program had ever seen. The reason I was bad was because I treated my internship as a free ticket to watch my hero perform live on stage every day, and not as a way to help the show run smoothly by doing errands. My boss, the script coordinator, greatly disliked me. Not only because I was bad at my job, but because hating everything was one of her personality traits. You know those people who legitimize their sarcastic, negative personalities by saying proudly they are "lifelong New Yorkers"? She was one of those. Her favorite catchphrase was "Are you on crack?" On my last day, she shook my hand limply and said a terse "Bye" without looking away from her J.Crew catalogue.

When I arrived in New York, I didn't even really know how to apply for the job. I had not kept in touch with anyone at *Late Night,* because even as a nineteen-year-old, I knew that no one wants to keep in touch with the intern. I had placed a lot of faith in Woody Allen's belief that 80 percent of success is just showing up. I said to myself: Are you *serious*? *80 percent*? Sure, I can just *show up*. Here I am, New York! Give me a job!

It turns out the other 20 percent is kind of the difficult, nebulous part.

I wrote a letter to NBC asking how I could submit sketches to be considered for *Late Night*. I got a letter back saying that the network could not even *open an envelope* that contained creative material that was not submitted by an agent. I thought the phrase "cannot even open the envelope" was a tad dramatic. NBC legal, you drama queens. This initial rejection served as NBC "negging" me, to borrow a phrase from my very favorite book, *The Game*. It worked. NBC became the sexy guy at the party I needed to be with. When I finally got with him, years later, sure, he was fourth place, kind of fat, balding, and a little worse for the wear, but I still got him.

Here I am, ruining my guest appearance on my hero's talk show
with dorky gesticulation.

HOME IS WHERE THE BED IS

I was jobless, but so were Brenda and Jocelyn. Together we rented a railroad-style apartment in Windsor Terrace, Brooklyn. The railroad apartment, for those of you who've never seen one, is styled after the sleek comfort of a 1930s industrial rail-road car. All the rooms are connected in a line, and you have to walk through one room to get to the next. Everything about it is awful, except if you need a set for a play that takes place during the Great Depression. The only people this intimate setup worked for were three female best friends who had no secrets from one another, were comfortable (enough) being walked in on naked, and had no boyfriends (or no boyfriends who were ever invited over). Enter us!

Real estate was our first disappointment in New York: we had set our sights on trendy Williamsburg, which had plenty of chic coffee shops, cool boutiques, and cute, straight guys. I knew I wouldn't have been able to afford those coffee shops and boutiques, or had the nerve to talk to any of those hipster guys, but I would have liked to be around them, and felt that it was plausible I could have that life. After visiting several basement-level tenements that were out of our price range, we settled for Windsor Terrace. When we moved there, Windsor Terrace was a Park Slope–adjacent mini-neighborhood that could've been the exterior set for much of *Welcome Back, Kotter*. Not grim, but not great. It was populated mostly by middle-age lesbian couples who had taken on the noble challenge of gentrifying the neighborhood.

Brenda and I shared the center bedroom and the single queen bed it would hold, and Jocelyn fashioned herself a sort of bohemian-chic burrow out of the last bedroom, which, while it was the only room with true privacy, was also the size of a handicapped bathroom. She installed a twin loft bed and hung a batik tapestry over the lofted area, where she would read books and magazines for hours. Jocelyn is the kind of person who goes into any room, sizes it up, and immediately tries to loft a bed there. To this day, she lives in an apartment with a loft bed.

This was a good arrangement because Jocelyn has hoarding tendencies, and some degree of containment was crucial. (Hoarding has pejorative connotations now, but you have to understand this was before the show *Hoarders* depicted hoarders as gruesome loners with psychological problems. Joce is a hoarder of the cheerful, social, Christmas-lights-year-round variety.) Jocelyn would save stacks of six-year-old magazines because there might be a recipe in one of them for jambalaya, which she would need someday if we threw a big Mardi Gras–themed dinner. (This wasn't crazy, because we would occasionally do things like that.) People who visited our apartment and saw her curtained lair probably assumed Jocelyn was a gypsy we had inherited as a condition of getting the apartment.

I was going through a phase where all my photos had me making a "whoo!" face.

And the stairs. Oh, the stairs. The staircase in our third-floor walk-up was the steepest, hardest, metal-est staircase I have ever encountered in my life. It was a staircase for killing someone and making it seem like an accident. Our downstairs neighbor was a toothless man, somewhere in his eighties or nineties. He lived with what seemed like two younger male relatives, with "younger" meaning in their sixties. In the dead of summer or winter they would wear those ribbed white tank tops grossly named wife beaters, which is how we knew they were rent-control tenants (if anyone wears year-round wife beaters, it is the same as saying they are enjoying the benefits of a rent-controlled apartment). They also spoke a language with one another that seemed like a hybridized version of an Eastern European language and the incomprehensible mumble of *Dick Tracy* henchmen. They would've been frightening, except they were incredibly timid and scared of *us* for some reason. Like when that monster in the *Bugs Bunny* cartoon gets scared of a mouse and runs screaming all the way back to his castle.

In the summer, feral cats in heat clung onto the screens of our living room, meowing mournfully until we threw a glass of water at them. When it got cold, the roaches migrated in and set up homes in every drain. Sometimes, when I got up in the middle of the night to use the bathroom, I would feel a disgusting crackly squelch under my foot, and I'd know I'd have to rinse off a roach from my heel. That was our apartment. We took the bad with the pretty good. Plus, we could afford it, Prospect Park wasn't too far, and people already assumed we were lesbians, so we fit into the neighborhood right away. It was all good.

Until we tried to pursue our dreams.

Jocelyn accompanies me on the subway to my first-ever open mike gig.

I AM TERRIBLE AT EVERYTHING

Everything I learned about trying to get hired as a comedy writer came from the Film and Television section of the Lincoln Center Barnes and Noble. I didn't have the money to buy many of the books there, so I spent hours sitting in the aisle, copying down sections in a loose-leaf notebook. I was not the worst offender. There were aspiring screenwriters sprawled all over the place there. They'd nurse a single coffee for hours. One kid I saw there all the time frequently brought a large pizza with him and ate the entire thing slowly while handwriting inquiry letters to literary agencies.* The only really valuable thing I learned from the Lincoln Center Barnes and Noble was that the only way I could get hired by a TV show was to write a "spec," or sample script, of a popular current show. That's when I started working on my first spec, a *Will & Grace* sample, having seen the show only a handful of times.

I went on one audition when I was in New York. I wasn't actively pursuing acting jobs, but this one was tailor-made for me. It was an open casting call for *Bombay Dreams,* an Andrew Lloyd Webber–produced musical extravaganza that was transferring from London to Broadway. I was encouraged by the relative lack of actresses, aged eighteen to thirty, who sang, lived in the tristate area, and also looked Indian. Nothing gives you confidence like being a member of a small, weirdly specific, hard-to-find demographic.

The first *Bombay Dreams* audition was a singing audition. I auditioned with "Somewhere Out There" from *An American Tail.* In the audition room I saw some Indian girls, but mostly Latina girls trying to pass for Indian. The audition sign-in sheet read like it was for a production of *West Side Story.*

---

* It is interesting to note that this Barnes and Noble no longer exists— perhaps no one was buying books there?

My singing audition went really well, mostly because they were relieved an actual Indian person was auditioning. On the way out, the casting assistant walked me all the way to the street, saying, "We were really so happy you made it out here." I nodded demurely, like I had a million other auditions that week that were more exciting than this one, and left. They were so *happy I made it out there?* Why not just hand me my start paperwork? On the subway I started planning what I would do when I got the job. First I would go to Dean & Deluca and buy some tiny marzipan candies in the shape of fruit, an expensive treat I noticed a lot of fancy-looking older white women buying. Next I would pay for an exterminator to come to our apartment to kill the cockroaches. After that I'd take Bren and Joce out to dinner at Le Cirque, like I was a creepy Wall Street sugar daddy and they were my pretty arm candy.

I got a callback for a dance audition. I had never danced in my life and did not know what to wear. I went to a dance clothing surplus outlet in Chelsea I'd seen ads for in the *PennySaver.* Their stuff was discounted because it was irregular, which means the colors were weird or some buttons were off. I bought brown tights, a sleeveless pink leotard, and a white iridescent skirt that wrapped around my waist and was fastened with Velcro. I capped off the entire look with some traditional pink ballet slippers. In the communal mirror of the dressing room of that surplus store, a young Asian girl trying on ballet clothes with her mom said, "Mommy, you should dress like that," *referring to me.* The mom hushed her in an Asian language. This sealed the deal. I had never felt more graceful in my life.

At the audition I looked like a fucking idiot. The other girls were all dressed in versions of what actual dancers wear: low-key black leggings, a tank top, and sneakers. I looked like the children's birthday party performer playing Angelina Ballerina, the ballet-dancing mouse. A Kevin Federline–looking choreographer taught us an incredibly complicated Bollywood dance routine, which we then had to perform on tape. I stumbled through it like a groggy teamster who had wandered into the wrong room backstage, breathing heavily and vaguely hitting my marks. KFed stopped me before the song was done and kindly asked if I needed some water. I laughed because, as everyone knows, laughing is a great way to disguise heavy breathing. I then exited on the pretense of getting a drink, and quickly left the building. It remains the single most embarrassing performance of my life, and it's on tape somewhere. I like to think Andrew Lloyd Webber watches it whenever he's feeling down.

My *Will & Grace* spec was a disaster. In an attempt to achieve the cheeky, gay-centric tone of the show, I had written a sample so over-the-top offensively gay that it actually reads like a propaganda sketch to incite antigay sentiment.

So things were coming together nicely for me to embark on a full-fledged depression. One good thing about New York is that most people function daily while in a low-grade depression. It's not like if you're in Los Angeles, where everyone's so actively working on cheerfulness and mental and physical health that if they sense you're down, they shun you. Also, all that sunshine is a cruel joke when you're depressed. In New York, even in your misery, you feel like you belong. But it was still hard to fail, so consistently, at everything I had once been Camilla Parker Bowles–level good at.

Brenda and I would fix that, but we didn't know it yet.

The Exact Level of Fame I Want

I OBVIOUSLY WANT to be super famous and for everyone to love me. That's why I got into this racket. It helps that I love writing jokes, but let's face it, that was just the means to an end.

Oftentimes when I'm in the writers' room at *The Office,* and it's 11:00 p.m., the script we're rewriting is halted because we're all waiting for our boss to approve an outfit for the character Pam that shoots the following day, and my mind wanders. First I wonder if I will ever get the opportunity to live in a tree house like the one in the *Swiss Family Robinson* house at Disneyland, where we'd have a giant seashell for a sink. After I realize that, no, that will never happen, I think about the exact amount of fame I want.

To me, the person with the best fame is Conan O'Brien. When I interned at *Late Night,* I thought, *Wow, this is the guy who has totally nailed being famous.* Nobody cared what he wore (some kind of dark-colored suit), his hair was famously always the same, and he got to sit at the same desk every episode. Clearly he was a hardworking genius, but he was the only famous person I saw who was always being himself. Everyone else had to be someone else. Conan did strange little comedy bits that were completely his style, interviewed celebrities who were much more dressed up than he was, and even got to do cooking demonstrations.

(When I interned there, I noticed he never ate the food during commercial breaks. I don't understand that level of discipline.)

I didn't want to be Regis or Kathie Lee, because their chairs were too high. I'm sorry, I'm supposed to sit like that for an hour? Too much blood rushing to my ankles. No, thanks.

Once I saw Paris Hilton leaving a restaurant in Hollywood and the paparazzi cameras were all over her. It looked so unpleasant. It wasn't because she didn't look sensational—she was that perfect combination of fashionable and slutty—it was because the paparazzi guys were shouting these insanely rude and intrusive questions at her. Like, asking her who she was sleeping with and stuff. I was kind of interested in the answer, so I was glad they asked, but it was still gross.

But then, behind Paris, I saw Sacha Baron Cohen quietly exit the restaurant completely unnoticed, walk up to the valet, get in his car, and drive away. Can you believe that? I mean, it's Sacha Baron Fuckin' Cohen! (Wasn't sure where to put the *fuckin'* in there, but I think I chose right.) None of the paparazzi had any idea who he was, but he was also, like Conan, one of the most respected living comedy icons in the world. And I thought, *Man, I want to be that famous.*

Here are some more ways I'd love to be famous (I am required to declare that these ideas are technically owned by NBC-Universal, because I imagined them while on their payroll).

I NEVER HAVE TO WAIT IN LINE FOR BRUNCH

Like everyone normal, I would never have a bumper sticker, ever. However, if I saw one that read, "Hell Is Waiting in Line for Brunch," I might buy a thousand and plaster my car with them. I'd like to be so famous that if I want to lazily eat out on a Sunday afternoon, someone whisks me past a long line of poor slobs waiting in the sun and to a private table.

I GET TO SEE THE LAKERS ALL THE TIME

Look, I don't need to have Jack Nicholson seats or what-ever—honestly, who needs to live in constant peril of a sweaty 7-foot-tall, 240-pound guy falling on you?—but I'd love to be so famous that people who do have amazing tickets would be psyched to have me come with them. I just want to sit close enough so that I can ask the Laker Girls questions about their makeup regimens.

TEENAGERS IDOLIZE MY "LOOK"

I was at Benefit Cosmetics picking up some lip glosses and try-ing to scam some free samples one Saturday a few months ago. While I was there, I saw two adorable ninth-grade girls getting makeovers for their semiformal, which was that night. They both had torn-out reference pictures of Emma Watson. When I was their age, I had done the same with pictures of Meg Ryan. I was obsessed with her edgy shag from the otherwise forgettable movie *Addicted to Love*. The edgy shag did not suit my face. If you must know, it made me look like a touring 1980's road comic. A male one.

Copying a celebrity's hairstyle is some enviable adoration right there. Since I don't think anyone will ever want my haircut, it'd have to be something else. Maybe kids would want my per-fectly hairless forearms.

IF I SUPPORT A CAUSE, I CAN ACTUALLY HELP IT

Sean Penn, like, lives in Haiti, right? That's too much. I can't do that. That's some hard-core goodness right there. But I'd love to make an enormous impact by being the vocal spokesperson for a cause, somewhere on the level of Mary Tyler Moore ending horse carriage rides in Central Park.

THE FASHION POLICE SLAUGHTER ME, CONSTANTLY, AND I DON'T CARE

There's a certain badass-ness to someone like Helena Bonham Carter, who just doesn't give a crap about what the Fashion Police say. And when I say the Fashion Police, of course I'm speaking of the small group of screeching gay guys and fashion "experts" on that E! show led by the reanimated corpse of Joan Rivers. Joan, actually, is still pretty great. One Emmy Awards show a few years ago, she said my dress made me look like I was going to the prom from hell. It traumatized my entire week, but even I had to admit that it was a funny thing to say. The point is, it only traumatized me because I *had the time* to be traumatized. I want to be so famous and busy that I only ever find these insults amusing, and chuckle at them good-naturedly before I get on my private jet to be a UN ambassador to Cameroon, or wherever.

BATSHIT STUFF I WEAR IS IMMEDIATELY CONSIDERED FASHIONABLE

Kind of related to what I've just said. I want to rock harem pants or black lipstick like Gwen Stefani does and have people be like, "That's just Mindy," and then everyone starts doing it.

WHEN I GET OLD, I'M A SIGHT GAG FOR TV SHOWS

I want to be so famous that people put me in their TV shows as the desiccated old broad who gets big laughs simply because no one has ever seen such an old bag of bones recite memorized lines, and because the sight of me brings up warm, nostalgic memories of their youth. Future hipsters will love me ironically.

I CAN NEVER GO TO JAIL

It'd be great to be so famous that if I murder someone, I will never, ever, ever serve any jail time, even if it's totally obvious to everyone that I did it.

I HAVE TO HAVE A PSEUDONYM

I read that Michael Jackson used to have prescriptions for Demerol under the alias Jack London. So much about Michael Jackson's life was tragic and strange, but that detail is just so cool. I like thinking that Michael Jackson was like, "Let's see, let's see. Who do I want to commemorate in my request for drugs? You know what? I always did love *White Fang*. Jack London it is." My alias for hotels and stuff would be Gwendolyn Trundlebed, a nonsense name I've always loved that my friend Mike Schur came up with during the third season of *The Office*.

MY STAND-IN GETS PLASTIC SURGERY TO LOOK MORE LIKE ME

In movies, actors will sometimes have a stand-in. The stand-in is an actor who is hired to stand in the place of another actor for lighting purposes, so the first actor can take a nap or go do drugs in his trailer. I worked on a movie once where the lead actor (a very famous actor whom I'll call Tony Dash) traveled with his personal stand-in. They were best friends. It is already weird to be best friends with someone who looks like you, but the absolute weirdest part was that the stand-in had gotten extensive facial plastic surgery to look more like Tony. I think he did it so that Tony would never, ever think of hiring anyone else to be his stand-in, and he'd have job security for the rest of his life. He looked like the half-melted version of this famous actor. It was horrifying and titillating at the same time. It just showed so much power. I want there to be some slightly grotesque version of me following me around on sets all over the world, and we hang out and vacation together.

KENAN THOMPSON PLAYS ME ON *SNL*

I can't tell whether I would hate this or love this so much. There are arguments for both. I'll say love it, for now.

Karaoke Etiquette

WITH THE EXCEPTION of Japanese businessmen, no one likes karaoke more than I do. When I graduated from college, my aunt Sreela and uncle Keith gave me the single best present I've ever received: a professional-level karaoke machine. I don't know if they were aiming to become my favorite aunt and uncle for all eternity, but that was the result. When I arrived in Brooklyn with Bren and Jocelyn, we set that machine up to our TV before we had a bed or couch. We'd just take turns belting Whitney Houston in an empty room, while the others sat Indian-style, impatiently waiting their turn.

Because we were unemployed for so much of those first months, and also because we are cheesy crooning hambones, we did a lot of karaoke. Now, in L.A., all the best birthday parties I go to take place in a karaoke bar or, for the true karaoke experience, a dark windowless box in Koreatown that smells faintly of Korean-style chicken wings. What follows are some things I think really maximize the karaoke experience.

When I pick songs for karaoke, I have three concerns: (1) What will this song say about me? (2) How will I sound singing it? and (3) How will it make people feel?

The key is that the third one matters the most, by a factor of a hundred. When most people sing karaoke, they think of themselves as contestants on *American Idol,* and they sing and perform their hearts out. But I really think people should be thinking of themselves more as temporary DJs for the party. It's kind of a responsibility. It's up to you to sing a kick-ass upbeat song that sets the mood for your friends to have fun, drink, and pick up girls and guys.

And it kind of behooves you to pick a short song. I don't care if Don freakin' McLean shows up in a red-white-and-blue tuxedo, no one is allowed to sing "American Pie." It's actually kind of hostile to a group of partiers to pick a song longer than three minutes.

Stray observations I would like to add: I like when small people sing big brassy songs, like, say, if my friend Ellie Kemper sings "Big Spender" in a booming voice. I also like when guys sing girls' songs, but not in a campy way. Like a guy earnestly singing "Something to Talk About" is wonderful. Guys sometimes do this thing where they sing a Britney or Rihanna song and do a campy impression of the singer, to be funny, and it's painful. An amazing thing to do is to pick a song that has lyrics in another language. That's why I tend to always sing Madonna's "La Isla Bonita" for karaoke. I would die if a guy sang a Gipsy Kings song. Die in a good way, obviously.

Day Jobs

IN OTHER PLACES in this book, you've seen the fruitless attempts I made while living in New York to pursue my goal of show business employment. This section is about my attempts to get day jobs. At first I called this chapter "Mama's Gots to Pay da Bills," but I thought that title made it sound like maybe I had been a stripper or had a brood of illegitimate children.

It was October 2001 and I lived in New York City. I was twenty-two. I, like many of my female friends, suffered from a strange combination of post-9/11 anxiety and height-of-*Sex-and-the-City* anxiety. They are distinct and unnerving anxieties. The questions that ran through my mind went something like this:

Should I keep a gas mask in my kitchen? Am I supposed to be able to afford Manolo Blahnik shoes? What is Barneys New York? You're trying to tell me a place called "Barneys" is fancy? Where are the fabulous gay friends I was promised? Gay guys hate me! Is this anthrax or powdered sugar? Help! Help!

The greatest source of stress was that it had been three months since I'd moved to New York and I still didn't have a job. You know those books called *From Homeless to Harvard* or *From Jail to Yale* or *From Skid Row to Skidmore*? They're these inspirational memoirs about young people overcoming the bleakest of circumstances and going on to succeed in college. I was worried I would be the subject of a reverse kind of book: a pathetic tale of a girl with a great education who frittered it away watching syndicated *Law & Order* episodes on a sofa in Brooklyn. *From Dartmouth to Dickhead* it would be called. I needed a job.

CARING FOR THE YOUNG AND EATING THEIR FOOD

By placing hundreds of neon green flyers all over the wealthiest neighborhoods in Brooklyn and Manhattan, I finally got a job babysitting. I was paying my $600 portion of the rent taking care of two adorable girls named Dylan and Haley. Dylan and Haley were from a wealthy family in Brooklyn Heights. Not wealthy in a simply went-to-private-school way. Wealthy in a each-had-her-own-floor-of-a-historic-brownstone-in-Brooklyn-Heights-and-wore-all-organic-clothing way. I guess "crazy loaded" is the more accurate way to say it. Their dad invented the Internet, or something like that (not Al Gore), and whenever I walked into their mansion on Pineapple Street, I always whispered to myself, *This is the house that inventing the Internet built.* Dylan and Haley's parents had divorced years before, and I never met Internet Inventor Dad. I only interacted with gorgeous Internet Inventor–Marrying Mom, who looked like a slightly older Alicia Keys. Internet Inventor–Marrying Mom hired me on nights when she went out on dates or had plans for a girls' night with her all-black, all-glamorous friends. Later I read that Internet Inventor Dad was seriously dating an internationally famous supermodel. They rolled high. If my babysitting stint were taking place now, they would have a dynasty of reality shows on Bravo, and I'd be the pixilated chaperone in a cable-knit sweater escorting the girls to Knicks courtside seats.

Once Internet Inventor–Marrying Mom gave me an unopened

bottle of Clinique *Happy* that someone had given her and she knew she'd never use. "It's not fancy or anything," she said sheepishly, as though she were handing me a bottle of *Lady Musk* by Walmart.

What is this world? I thought. *Clinique isn't fancy anymore?*

I was a little worried about babysitting at first, because though I have the voice of an eleven-year-old girl, I have no natural rapport with children. I'm not one of those women who melts when a baby enters the room and immediately knows all the right age-specific questions to ask. I always assume the wrong things and offend someone. "Does he speak yet? Does what he says make sense, or is it still gurgle-babble?" Also, I'm always worried I'm going to accidentally scratch the kid with my fingernail or something. I'm the one who looks at the infant, smiles nervously, and as my contribution to small talk, robotically announces to the parent, "Your child looks healthy and well cared for."

So it was surprising that I killed it as a babysitter. Er, maybe "killed it" is a wrong and potentially troubling way to express what I'm trying to say. The point is, I was an excellent babysitter. It helped that the kids thought I was a genius. It was so easy to seem like a genius to Dylan and Haley when helping them with their homework. For instance, one night, I explained that the mockingbird in the title of *To Kill a Mockingbird* was actually a symbol for the character Boo Radley. Dylan looked at me with wonder. "Why are you babysitting us?" she asked. "Why aren't you teaching at a college?"

I also knew what little girls want to talk about, which is boy bands. Haley and I would talk for hours about which member of 'N Sync we'd want to marry. After long deliberation, the answer was always J. C. Chasez. Joey Fatone's last name was going to be "Fat One" no matter how great he was, and even though they didn't know at their age that Lance Bass was gay outright, they sensed he'd make a better good friend and confidante. As for Justin Timberlake, well, JT was the coolest and hottest, but too flashy, so we couldn't trust him to be faithful. J. C. Chasez was the smart compromise. We would talk like this, in complete unironic seriousness, for hours. The reason I was better than other babysitters was that I would never rush them. In me they had an open-minded listener to every pro and con of spending the rest of their lives with each band member of 'N Sync. I may have gotten more out of it than they did.

When the kids went to bed, the real fun began: me turning on *Showtime at the Apollo* in their tricked-out den and going to town on all the kid-friendly snack food in the house. Kid-friendly food is the best, because kid-friendly simply means "total garbage." I ate frozen chicken nuggets shaped like animals, fruit chews shaped like fruit, and fruits shaped like cubes in syrup. I discovered that kids hate for any food to resemble the form it originally was in nature. They are on to something because that processed garbage was insanely delicious. I spent some excellent Saturday nights watching Mo'Nique strutting onstage at the Apollo while I ate a handful of children's chewable vitamins and wrapped myself up in my boss's cashmere kimono. I did it so much that it became a problem. One evening after her bath, Haley pulled me aside, wracked with guilt: "Mommy wanted to know who ate all the turtle-shaped bagel pizzas, and I knew it was you, but I lied and said it was me." She burst into tears. I hugged her and told her, "You can never tell her the truth." And then I let her stay up an extra hour watching *Lizzie McGuire*. Bribes and boy bands. That's all you need to be a babysitter.

Babysitting did not pay the bills or give me health insurance, which I guess is good, because otherwise I would probably be an au pair somewhere right now. I needed to get a real job.

NETWORK PAGE DREAMS

The page program at the network TBN is very prestigious, and famously harder to get into than Harvard. No, TBN is not the real name of the network, but there is an old saying, "Don't bite the hand that feeds you," which applies here. The TBN page program turns ambitious, overeducated twentysomethings into friendly, uniformed butlers. I wasn't sure it was really my style, but it seemed like the first rung on the ladder to somehow working in TV. Young television writers all aspire to be TBN pages, in the hope that a late-night talk show host like Craig Ferguson or David Letterman will eventually overhear them uttering something witty while leading a tour, and then say, "You're brilliant! Why don't you come work for me and be my best friend?" They hire only seventy or eighty pages a year, out of something like forty-two million applicants. I decided the odds were stacked against me, which strangely made me feel like I was going to get the job even more. Sports movies had brainwashed me into the belief that when the chips are down the most, that is when success is the most inevitable.

I'm the kind of person who would rather get my hopes up really high and watch them get dashed to pieces than wisely keep my expectations at bay and hope they are exceeded. This quality has made me a needy and theatrical friend, but has given me a spectacularly dramatic emotional life.

Anyway, I got called in for an interview with the program. I wore a pin-striped skirt suit I ordered from the clothing section of the Victoria's Secret catalogue. You know that section, where they can make a woman modeling a pair of overalls look slutty? Yeah, it's amazing.

I thought I looked pretty awesome—like one of Ally McBeal's friends in cheaper material.

I arrived fifteen minutes early for my interview, which was

the first of my three mistakes. I was interviewed by a paunchy and balding man name Leon. He was one of the guys who managed the page program, and it was obvious that lunchtime was his thirty-minute respite from this hell job of interviewing an assembly line of ambitious, obnoxious liberal arts school grads. He didn't have an assistant to tell me to wait outside. There was no "outside" to his tiny office. Or a waiting area, as I thought there would be. It wasn't a posh enough job to have earned him all these extra rooms. My early arrival meant that either he would have to interview me or I would have to wander around Midtown for a while. Unfortunately, he chose the former. He reluctantly shoved his Quiznos sub aside and told me to have a seat. Strike one.

Life had been hard on Leon, his portliness and baldness obscuring his relative youth. Looking at a photo on his desk of him with two little kids, I asked, "Oh, are those your kids? They're so cute."

He looked aghast. "I'm twenty-five. Those are my nephews. You think I have kids?"

I was unable to conceal my surprise. "Oh! It's just that, you don't look, um, you seem more mature than that."

Leon gestured to me. "We're basically the same age."

Without thinking, I immediately responded, "Well, I'm actually three years younger than you." Why on earth did I correct him on his point? Oh, because I was a snotty little idiot.

Strike two.

Leon asked me, while eyeing his Quiznos sandwich longingly, why I wanted to be a TBN page. I answered honestly, saying that I would be honored to work for a terrific company that had been host to all my favorite shows growing up, and that the opportunities that came from the page program seemed amazing.

"Hold on." Leon stopped me. "So you only want this job for the opportunities it *affords?*"

I was puzzled. "I mean, that's part of why I'm applying, yes."

"This job is more than just a stepping-stone." Leon jotted down a short word on my résumé that could only have been *hate* or *yuck*. Strike three.

Leon was now openly disgusted. What had he wanted? For me to say that all I wanted to do into my twilight years was give people backstage tours of morning talk shows? Oh, yeah. Yes. That's exactly what he wanted me say. I left knowing with certainty that I had not gotten the job. It was hard to be devastated, because it had been such a top-to-bottom disaster.

Now when I watch my friend Jack McBrayer excellently portray Kenneth, the career NBC page on *30 Rock,* I understand what kind of commitment Leon wanted from me. I wonder if Leon is a consultant for the show. Or still a page.

I WORK FOR A TV PSYCHIC

Still babysitting, with no health insurance, I began to become a germaphobe, because I could not afford to get sick and go to the hospital. From a friend of a friend, I landed an interview for an entry-level job as a production assistant on a show I'll call *Bridging the Underworld with Mac Teegarden.* This was a cable program featuring the psychic Mac Teegarden, who relayed messages to members of the studio audience from their dead friends and relatives.

The morning I interviewed for the job, I had an enormous pimple on my face. A giant pimple is bad news for everyone, but if you have dark brown skin and a huge whitehead in the center of your forehead, it is especially disgusting. It wasn't even one of those stoic pimples that goes quietly when you pop it; this one was cystic and painful and had roots that seemed to extend into my brain. I wanted to postpone my interview but it would have been a last-minute change, and I wanted to hide the fact that I was a vain flake for as long as I could. (Coincidentally, Vain Flake is the name of my perfume, available at your finer drugstores and coastal Kmarts.) So, with my zit throbbing like a nightclub, I went to the interview.

My interview was with a segment producer named Gail and the exec producer Sally. Sally was a stout, masculine-looking woman, but not unattractive. She reminded me of a blond Rosie O'Donnell in her height: appealing, confident, and a tiny bit brusque.

They were both very nice, and seemed highly concerned about filling a position made vacant by their last PA, who had left abruptly for Teach for America. (Thank you, Teach for America! Luring away America's finest minds so that the rest of us can snatch up their jobs.) My interview lasted eight minutes. I could type, I could get coffee, I didn't have an accent. I guess Old Throbby on my forehead was my lucky charm!

Working for a TV psychic was not what my parents envisioned after investing in my degree, but the job had health benefits, and this pleased my mother. My mother is a doctor, and somewhat of a militant on the subject of health benefits, which is why I may seem slightly obsessed with them. The description of the PPO was more exciting than the job itself. I was working at a job that was vaguely in the world of television making $500 a week! Cue Madonna's "Holiday"! It's margarita time!

I always thought mediums were supposed to be old crones with glass eyes of the *Drag Me to Hell* variety, but Mac Teegarden turned out to be a wildly normal guy. He was a thirty-ish former phlebotomist and ballroom dance instructor with a Long Island accent. He was attractive in a Mario Lopez way, with slicked-back hair and a wardrobe of tight long-sleeve T-shirts. He looked like the kind of guy who lifts weights twice a day, is a great husband, and goes to Manhattan nightclubs with his wife four months after Justin Timberlake went there. I liked him a lot.

My immediate boss was Gail, the one who'd interviewed me. Gail was forty, single, and loved the world created by *Sex and the City* more passionately than any other person I knew; I think she would've disappeared into the show if she could have. (Let me take a moment here to stress again just how pervasive the *Sex and the City* culture was in New York in 2002. You could be an NYU freshman, a Metropolitan Transit Authority worker, or an Orthodox Jewish woman living in a yeshiva: you watched *Sex and the City*.) Without knowing me at all, Gail nicknamed me Minz. I respond very well to people being overly familiar with me a little too soon. It shows effort and kindness. I try to do this all the time. It makes me feel part of a big, familial, Olive Garden-y community.

Gail would talk at length on Mondays about *Sex and the City* (the day after the show aired) and how it perfectly mirrored her life. I could tell she wanted to have a TV-show-worthy Manhattan existence, and I knew I was a disappointment to her when I failed to fill the adorable minority sidekick role. (By the way, I in no way mean to impugn the fun job of minority sidekick. Minority sidekicks always get to wear Hawaiian shirts and Tevas and stuff. I would gladly be the Indian female version of what Rob Schneider is to Adam Sandler, to just about anyone.)

"How is your love life, Minz?" she would ask hungrily, hoping to be entertained by raunchy details.

I had none. "Um, you know. So hard to meet guys," I answered vaguely, hoping my lack of a sex life would seem mysterious and not pathetic.

"You're such a Charlotte," she replied. Gail found lemons and made lemonade. That's the one nice thing about being a dork about men: you can sometimes play it off as restrained and classy.

Gail loved to talk about how stressed she was. She would do this thing where we'd be walking in the hallway, and suddenly she'd stop in her tracks, rub both of her temples with her index and middle fingers, and theatrically let out a deep guttural moan: "Mooog."

"Mooog. Minz. I am just so stressed out," she'd say. "I just want to go home, open a bottle of red wine, draw up a hot bath, light some candles, and listen to David Gray."

A note about me: I do not think stress is a legitimate topic of conversation, in public anyway. No one ever wants to hear how stressed out anyone else is, because most of the time *everyone is stressed out.* Going on and on in detail about how stressed out I am isn't conversation. It'll never lead anywhere. No one is going to say, "Wow, Mindy, you really have it *especially* bad. I have heard some stories of stress, but this just *takes the cake.*"

This is entirely because my parents are immigrant professionals, and talking about one's stress level was just totally outlandish to them. When I was three years old my mom was in the middle of her medical residency in Boston. She had been a practicing obstetrician and gynecologist in Nigeria, but in the United States she was required to do her residency all over again. She'd get up at 4:00 a.m. and prepare breakfast, lunch, and dinner for my brother and me, because she knew she wouldn't be home in time to have dinner with us. Then she'd leave by 5:30 a.m. to start rounds at the hospital. My dad, an architect, had a contract for a building in New Haven, Connecticut, which was two hours and forty-five minutes away. It would've been easier for him to move to New Haven for the time of the construction of the building, but then who would have taken care of us when my mom was at the hospital at nights? In my parents' vivid imaginations, lack of at least one parent's supervision was a gateway to drugs, kidnapping, or at the very minimum, too much television watching. In order to spend time with us and save money for our family, my dad dropped us off at school, commuted the two hours and forty-five minutes every morning, and then returned in time to pick us up from our after-school program. Then he came home and boiled us hot dogs as an after-school snack, even though he was a vegetarian and had never eaten a hot dog before. In my entire life, I never once heard either of my parents say they were stressed. That was just not a phrase I grew up being allowed to say. That, and the concept of "Me time."

It is remarkable that I worked in the administrative offices of *Bridging the Underworld* without ever fully examining whether I believed that what Mac was doing was real. My only interaction with Mac Teegarden involved working for his producers. If you've never seen the show, Mac enters a room with a studio audience and asks questions that are presented as information he has received by communicating with dead relatives or dead friends of people in the audience. After he contacted the dead, he'd relay a message, and the show was over. Then a producer would pull that particular audience member aside, interview him further, and create a segment around him. I was one of the assistants who scurried around the selected audience member, collecting photos and getting him or her to sign releases.

When the audience members went back home, some of them would continue to call me. They saw me as the messenger's messenger. I have to admit that it was far more interesting to play a psychic conduit than it was to scan photos all day long. I spent hours talking to people, uninterrupted, about their loved ones who had passed away. I had no new psychic information, but I was someone new to talk to and confide in. I was great at it, and it became the best part of my day. It was strangely a lot like baby-sitting. People wanted to talk to me about what interested them, and I was good at listening to them and not telling them to stop talking. This would come in handy for me later when I became a producer on *The Office*.

If I had to testify under oath, I would admit, no, I don't believe Mac Teegarden is psychic. I've just been made too aware of people like Carl Sagan and basic science and stuff. I am certain, though, that Mac Teegarden provided an enormous amount of comfort to people who had unexpectedly lost loved ones. I don't know if it was psychic, but it was cathartic, and therapeutic, and it helped people.

MINDY KALING, SEXUAL HARASSER

I was living in Brooklyn with Brenda and Jocelyn, but *Bridging the Underworld* was taped in Queens. If I took the nicer subway, it meant I had to go through Manhattan every morning to get there, and that took a really long time. The subway line that ran the short way was the G line, which stopped exclusively in Brooklyn and Queens. That might be the only time the word *exclusive* has been used to describe the G train. At that time, the G train wasn't so hot. (My apologies to the train. I'm sure it's amazing now, with, like, a community garden and charter school in it. But not then.)

My coworker Rachel also lived in Brooklyn and took the G with me. Rachel was a pretty Jewish girl my age who was the heiress to a gourmet pickled Jewish food dynasty in L.A. She was an amazing cook who made her own bagels—a supremely cocky thing to do in New York—and other delicious food. When I went over to her house to watch TV, there would be homemade rugelach for snacks.

Rachel and I jokingly (and hilariously) called the G the Rape Train. One morning at work we were joking about it in the commissary. We did not see Sally, the producer, standing a few feet away.

"Did you hear the Rape Train added new stops?" I said to Rachel.

"Yeah? What are they?" she asked.

"Lurk, Stalk, Stab, and Dump Body," I said, very pleased with myself. Rachel laughed. We high-fived.

Suddenly, Sally appeared behind us. She looked really upset.

"Do you girls feel unsafe when you come to work in the morning?" Sally asked.

I was surprised she'd heard us. When you're that low on the totem pole, you sometimes think you're so unimportant that no one can hear you. My sense of invisibility had made me loose-lipped.

We hastily assured her that it was just our unfunny, pejorative nickname for the train, and that, based on the empirical evidence we had gathered so far, real rapists didn't traditionally attack two girls at once at seven in the morning, and that we were the real creeps, and we were sorry.

Sally looked displeased. "It's not a very funny thing to joke about," she said. "It's extremely inappropriate." She turned and left.

We were horrified. Later that morning, Rachel and I both got notes saying Sally wanted to see us in her office.

"She's going to fire us for sexual harassment!" Rachel worried.

I was freaked out. Sexual harassment was a real thing. You can't just joke about rape at work. We had endured a lengthy sexual harassment seminar on how fireable this behavior was. Sarah Silverman could make jokes about rape because, the fact of the matter was, she was much funnier and cuter than us. This was the problem of living in a post–Sarah Silverman world: lots of young women holding the scepter of inappropriateness did not know how to wield it.

I began wondering what I would tell my parents about getting fired. It would be embarrassing, especially since I had just bought my mother an expensive pair of Uggs with my new money. They were "I've Made It!" Uggs. I didn't know how I would tell them. I figured I could conceivably go three weeks without their noticing, living off graduation cash my aunt and uncle had given me. After that, I was toast.

When we were called in, we found Sally waiting with Joel, the head of Human Resources. Joel had a really tough job, because, as anyone knows, it's absolutely terrifying when someone from Human Resources is meeting you for any professional reason. Even if Joel simply wanted to share your table in the break room to enjoy a cup of coffee, you cringed a little. "Oh God, is Joel going to tell me my dental care is no longer covered?" I pretty much could only handle Joel for the ten minutes he was sitting with me going over my start paperwork. Then I never wanted to see him again. He's a lot like the Toby character from *The Office*.

Our situation looked bad. Now we would not only get fired and escorted immediately out of the building by security, but what we'd done would go in our Permanent Files, following us from job interview to job interview, ruining our careers.

"Girls," Sally said, "I took what you said very seriously this morning."

I was already making distancing body language from Rachel in my chair. I didn't want them to think we were attached at the hip. *You could fire Rachel and keep me! I'm a minority!*

"We want a town car to transport you to and from work. We can't have you be unsafe."

I couldn't believe it. Being potentially litigious young women had just landed us free car service to and from work, as though we were investment bankers. My inappropriate, unfunny remarks were getting us special treatment rather than fired. I felt like Ferris Bueller.

It actually cost the studio more to transport us by town car than it did to pay us. Everyone was instantly jealous. People began sucking up to us, hoping to wheedle a ride home in our town car. I treated that car like an interborough shuttle for all my friends. This is when I learned that crime pays. *From Dartmouth to Dirtbag!*

Best Friend Rights and Responsibilities

FOR ALMOST EIGHT years I lived with my best friends in either a cramped college dorm room or a small Brooklyn apartment. Normally these are the circumstances that drive one roommate to get engaged to some random guy super fast because she is so annoyed with her living situation. We managed it well, however, because we maintained an informal best friend code of conduct. I've outlined its most vital aspects here.

I CAN BORROW ALL YOUR CLOTHES

Anything in your closet, no matter how fancy, is co-owned by me, your best friend. I can borrow it for as long as I want. If I get something on it or lose it, I should make all good faith attempts to get it cleaned or buy you a new one, but I don't need to do that, and you still have to love me. If I ruin something of yours and don't replace it, you're allowed to talk shit about me to our other friends for one calendar year. That's it. Then you have to get over it. One stipulation to my borrowing your clothes is that you have to have worn the item at least once before I borrow it. I'm not a monster.

WE SLEEP IN THE SAME BED

If we're on a trip or if our boyfriends are away, and there's a bed bigger than a twin, we're partnering up. It is super weird for us not to share a bed. How else will we talk until we fall asleep?

I MUST BE 100 PERCENT HONEST ABOUT HOW YOU LOOK, BUT GENTLE

Your boyfriend is never going to tell you that your skirt is too tight and riding up too high on you. In fact, you shouldn't even have asked him, poor guy. He wants to have sex with you no matter how pudgy you are. I am the only person besides your mom who has the right (and responsibility) to tell you that. I should never be overly harsh when something doesn't look good on you, because I know you are fragile about this, and so am I. I will employ the gentle, vague expression "I'm not crazy about that on you," which should mean to you "Holy shit, take that off, that looks terrible!" I owe it to you to give feedback like a cattle prod: painful but quick.

I CAN DITCH YOU, WITHIN REASON

I can ditch you to hang out with a guy but *only* if that possibility has been discussed and getting-a-ride-home practicalities have been worked out, prior to the event. In return, I need to talk about you a lot with that guy so he knows how much I love you.

I WILL TAKE CARE OF YOUR KID IF YOU DIE

I can't even write about this, it's too sad. But yes, I will do that. And you will have one awesome little kid who hears endless stories about how amazing and beautiful and perfect you were. Incidentally, your kid will grow up loving Indian food.

I WILL NURSE YOU BACK TO HEALTH

If you are crippled with pain because of a UTI, I need to haul ass to CVS to get you some medicine, fast. I should also try to pick up a fashion magazine and the candy you like, because distracting you from your pain is part of nursing you back to health.

WE WILL TRADE OFF BEING SOCIAL ACTIVITIES CHAIR FOR OUR OUTINGS

On trips together, I promise to man up and be the person who drives the rental car sometimes, or uses my credit card and has people pay me back later. Someone needs to check on Yelp to see what the good brunch place is. Neither of us gets to be the princess all the time. I get that.

I WILL KEEP YOUR FAVORITE FEMININE HYGIENE PRODUCT AT MY HOUSE

Even though no one uses maxipads anymore, like you do, weirdo, I will keep a box at my house for when you come over.

SAME WITH YOUR CONTACT LENS SOLUTION

I can't believe you won't get Lasik already. You can afford it. I know you read someone went blind from it, but that was like twenty years ago. Not getting Lasik at this point is like being that girl in 2006 who didn't have a cell phone.

I WILL TRY TO LIKE YOUR BOYFRIEND FIVE TIMES

This is a fair number of times to hang out with your boyfriend and withhold judgment.

WHEN I TAKE A SHOWER AT YOUR PLACE, I WON'T DROP THE TOWEL ON THE FLOOR

Your home isn't a hotel. I forget sometimes because you make it so comfortable for me.

IF YOU'RE DEPRESSED, I WILL BE THERE FOR YOU

As everyone knows, depressed people are some of the most boring people in the world. I know this because when I was depressed, people fled. Except my best friends.

I will be there for you during your horrible break-up, or getting fired from your job, or if you're just having a bad couple of months or year. I will hate it and find you really tedious, but I promise I won't abandon you.

IF OUR PHONE CONVERSATION GETS DISCONNECTED, THERE'S NO NEED TO CALL BACK

I get it. You get it. We take forever getting off the phone anyway. This was a blessing.

I WILL HATE AND RE-LIKE PEOPLE FOR YOU

But you can't get mad if I can't keep track. Robby? Don't we hate him? No, we love him. Okay, okay. Sorry.

IT IS OKAY TO TAKE ME FOR GRANTED

I know when you fall in love with someone that you will completely forget about me. That hurts my feelings, but it is okay. Please try to remember to text me, if you can, if you know I have something going on in my life, like a work promotion or something.

NO TWO PEOPLE ARE BETTER THAN US

We fucking rock. No one can beat us.

Matt & Ben & Mindy & Brenda

I WAS FINALLY paying my bills, but Brenda and I weren't
doing anything creative. I became increasingly worried I had
moved to New York City to be a professional au pair. Because no
one was hiring us to act or write, Brenda and I decided to create
something to perform in ourselves. There was a one-hour window
per day when I could write with her. She left for her job as a public
school substitute teacher in the early morning and got back home
at 3:00 p.m. I left for my babysitting job at 4:00 p.m. and returned
between midnight and 1:00 a.m. So between 3:00 and 4:00 in the
afternoon, we met at the apartment to write. Unfortunately, we
didn't make great use of this one hour. Often we ended up lying
on the sofa watching Judge Judy scream at people for a while.

More often than not, our hour work session played out like
this:

INT. WINDSOR TERRACE APARTMENT LIVING ROOM, 3:10 P.M.

Bren is at the computer in my bedroom eating Honey Nut Cheerios from the
box. I am sitting on the bed, near her, eating a large piece of raw salmon I
bought from the supermarket. It was my homemade salmon "sashimi," deli-
cious and a fraction of the price it would be at a sushi restaurant, though not
at all safe. Bren looks up from the computer screen.

BREN: What do we want to do? What do we want to say?

ME: I think there should be only two characters, so we don't have to pay anyone.

Bren types this. Pause.

BREN: Do you want to go watch the *Jamie Kennedy Experiment?*

ME: Totally.

This went on for months. We could spend the entire hour arguing about the plausibility of Harry Potter and not write a single word.

In the early 2000s, the actors Matt Damon and Ben Affleck loomed large in our lives. They loomed large in everyone's lives, actually. This was the height of Bennifer. Sorry, I hate to resuscitate that term, which the media has thankfully put to bed, but it's important to remember what a phenomenon it was. It was like Pippa Middleton plus Beyoncé's legs times the latest Apple product. Bennifer was so big it was as though two people had never been in love before, and they had discovered it. I think it's also easy to forget that Bennifer created the trend of the blended celebrity couple name. Without Bennifer we wouldn't have Brangelina or Tomkat, or even the less used Jabrobra (James Brolin and Barbra Streisand). That is the gift that Ben Affleck and Jennifer Lopez gave us that has withstood the test of time.

Brenda and I have always done "bits," even before we knew they were called "bits." Bits are essentially "nonsense time" or, to describe it more pejoratively, "fucking around." We would take on characters, acting like them for a while on the way to the subway, or getting ready to go out. For whatever reason, around this time our favorite recurring bit was when Bren played Matt Damon and I was Ben Affleck. We played the "guys" very naturalistically, but they had a slightly jock-like, dude posture, and slightly lower voices. Again, have I emphasized how well we fit into our lesbian neighborhood?

Soon, our Matt and Ben had a rich and completely made-up backstory and dynamic. They had private jokes and shared memories: again, all made up. We did no research on the actual people, because we didn't care about their actual pasts; the real Matt Damon and Ben Affleck were simply jumping-off points for *our* Matt and Ben. It was a special kind of fun to be two best friends playing two other best friends.

Once we had characters, albeit nutty ones, we gained focus. If I can give one bit of advice to any drama major, high school theater kid, or inmate who is reading this in a prison library with dreams of being cast in the prison play, it's this: write your own part. It is the only way I've gotten anywhere. It is much harder work, but sometimes you have to take destiny into your own hands. It forces you to think about what your strengths really are, and once you find them, you can showcase them, and no one can stop you. I wasn't going to be able to showcase what I did best in an Off-Off-Broadway revival of *Our Town*. I was going to do it playing Ben Affleck. The premise for *Matt & Ben* is weird but simple: the script for *Good Will Hunting* falls from the ceiling of twenty-one-year-old Ben Affleck's apartment while the two are working on a screen adaptation of *The Catcher in the Rye*. They stop work and wonder about the significance of what has happened. The tone is somewhere between *The X-Files* and *The Odd Couple*. Here is one of the first scenes we wrote. Matt has arrived late to meet Ben, who is annoyed at him. Matt is late because he was auditioning for a play.

> MATT
> And I went, I had to go to this thing first, and then I came here.
>
> BEN
> What thing?

MATT

Nothing, just this audition thing.

BEN

For what?

MATT

For nothing. You don't know Shepard? Sam Shepard?

BEN

Yeah, of course.

MATT

You do?

BEN

Yeah, he was in *The Pelican Brief*, I love that guy. With the wrinkles? Is he in the play?

MATT

Uh, no he wrote the play, this play called "Buried Child." Won a Pulitzer. Anyway, it was nothing. It didn't happen.

BEN

What didn't happen? The audition?

MATT

No, I don't know. We'll see.

BEN

What's the part?

MATT

Vince.

BEN

No, what *kind* of part? Is it good?

MATT

Yeah. They were looking for a blonde.

BEN

A dark blonde? Cause you're not blonde.

We entered the play in the New York International Fringe Festival. Jocelyn and our friend Jason produced it, and we sold out every show. I think it was largely because of our tireless grassroots marketing. By grassroots, I mean, of course, environmentally destructive pestlike papering of the entire boroughs of Manhattan and Brooklyn. Each of us took stacks of postcards and put them in every diner, indie record store, and frites shop we could. (This was in that eight-month window in 2002 where frites were incredibly popular.)

We didn't want to pay a director to direct the show, so Bren and I directed it ourselves. It was a given that we would also star in it, not just because it was fun, but because, again, we didn't want to pay anyone. Our cheapness was the recurring source of our creative decisions. The set was minimal and we wore guys' clothes that we'd borrowed from Brenda's brothers, Jeff and Terry. We had no idea what we were doing, but we had a *purpose* after two years of living in New York and not having one. *Matt & Ben* was a respite from helplessness.

In 2002, the Fringe Festival named us Best Play of all five hundred shows. *The New Yorker* wrote of the show: "Goofy, funny, and improbably believable . . . Kaling and Withers have

created one of the most appealing male-bonding stories since Damon and Pythias. Or Oscar and Felix." That quote was easy to access because I have it tattooed on my clavicle.

This is when our lives started to change.

Producers got in touch with us to transfer the show to Off-Broadway. We got a director, we got a budget, and we could finally return our costumes to Brenda's brothers. The show went up at P.S. 122, a beautiful theater in the East Village that at one point had been a public school. There's a special level of cool for buildings in Manhattan that have at one point been something else. Someone might say to you, knowingly, "Oh, did you know this theater used to be a zipper factory?" or "You obviously know this discotheque used to be church, right?" or "We are eating in a restaurant that at one point was a typhoid containment center." That's what I love about New York. If Rikers Island ever goes under, I know André Balazs will have that place turned into a destination hotel for urban metrosexuals within a month, tops. People will sit in their cell/hotel rooms and say, "You know a convicted sex offender used to live in this cell, right?" The solitary confinement unit will be the honeymoon suite.

The show was short enough that we could do two shows a night. That in itself was challenging, because in the play, the twenty-one-year-old Ben tries to impress Matt by chugging an entire twelve-ounce bottle of apple juice in one gulp. So I actually gulped two bottles a night, though the apple juice was diluted. As I've written about in great detail in this book, I'm no dainty girl, but I'm a not a camel, either, and doing that twice in one evening was pretty nauseating.

Word of mouth from the Fringe helped sales. Nicole Kidman and Steve Martin coincidentally came to see the show on the same night, and before long the show was selling out so much that we had to add a third performance a night. This meant three bottles of diluted apple juice. By the third curtain call of

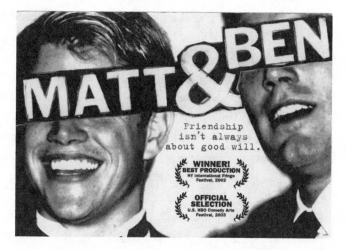

the night I had to consciously tell myself not to barf when we took our bows. I have never been so excited to hold back vomit.

BLOODSHED

On the night that Bruce Weber of the *New York Times* was reviewing the show, I accidentally punched Brenda in the face and broke her nose.

How does one accidentally fracture the face of one's best friend? Well, in my defense, there is a fight sequence in the play. It happens toward the very end. Matt has been so antagonized by Ben's immaturity that he tells him he has no talent. Ben, in the heat of the moment, punches Matt. It was a choreographed punch that we had worked on for weeks. But, I don't know, maybe I was drunk on apple juice, because my fist connected with her nose. It made a funny little cracking noise, which, I should probably note that Brenda did not immediately recognize as funny. That's because Brenda was too busy bleeding. Her shirt was instantly soaked with blood. Noses, for the record, bleed like crazy. It looked like I had stabbed her in the face. The audience collectively gasped; there was a long beat of confused silence during which Bren looked at the blood on her hand and then up at me. Then the house manager turned on the lights, and Brenda ran offstage.

Brenda held paper towels to her bleeding face, and I stood by her dumbly, completely in shock at what I had done. Our director David Warren appeared backstage moments later. He walked over to us briskly, with the imperturbable cool of a soldier who dismantles explosives for a living: "You have to finish. The show must go on. Go." There was no pussyfooting or assessing our comfort levels. We just had to do it. I had never heard anyone say the phrase "the show must go on" in the literal sense.

Brenda wrapped a makeshift bandage around her nose and valiantly went back onstage. We finished the last ten minutes of the play, took a bow to a standing ovation from an impressed, if horrified crowd, then jumped in a cab and headed to the emergency room of St. Vincent's. Bren's nose was officially broken. Years later, she acquiesced, it took her a weekend to not be mad at me anymore, but I think it was actually a full week before she forgave me. I don't blame her, though, Bren had a perfect nose. It's still pretty perfect, but now it has a tiny bump in it, which she good-naturedly pretends she likes. I guess the lesson is that if you're going to punch someone in the face, your best bet is to punch your best friend. Counterintuitive, I know.

Bruce Weber gave us a great review in the *Times* and also a separate little write-up about the nose incident. The publicity drove sales even more. People were curious about this weird, sixty-minute East Village play starring cross-dressers, during which at any moment physical violence might erupt. Great press from *Rolling Stone* and *Time* gave the producers confidence that the show could move to Los Angeles. So while there was a production going on at P.S. 122, we started another one in L.A.

EMOTIONAL BLOODSHED

Matt & Ben was invited to the U.S. Comedy Arts Festival, in Aspen, which was a big deal, because HBO sponsored the festival and the place was full of powerful Hollywood execs. Only later I would realize that someone wasn't powerful simply because they had the title of "exec" and a company had paid for him to travel. Actually, the fact that he could be shipped away from Los Angeles for a week meant he was *less* powerful.

Aspen looked the way I had always imagined Switzerland to be, down to the beautiful blonde women walking around in shearling coats with fur pom-poms. Aspen is one of those places that looks rustic but where everything is actually sickeningly expensive. This was on a whole other level from New York, which was just plain old grossly expensive. Aspen was so expensive I was surprised it wasn't entirely populated with the children of Middle Eastern oil moguls. We were put up at a Days Inn–style motel on the edge of town, but made the smart decision, upon waking up in the morning, of moving our hang-out time to the lobbies of the fanciest hotels. One day, we snuck into the gym at the St. Regis and did the elliptical machines for twenty exhilarating, frightening minutes.

How do I say that audiences in Aspen completely hated our show without you thinking I'm exaggerating? They hated the show. This was a festival designed for stand-up comedy and sketches, and we were the only play, which made us the longest show by a good thirty minutes. Even worse, we were in an auditorium so huge it could've doubled as a venue to announce the NFL draft. What worked so well in the intimacy of an Off-Broadway black box theater lost its charm in this cavernous space. It was like staging a flea circus at the Rose Bowl. Though, come to think of it, "flea circus" probably better describes the attention span of our audiences. People kept getting up to leave in the middle of the play. We'd hear the door open, light would stream in, and then we'd hear the conversation the leavers would have with the people waiting in line for the act scheduled to follow us. *When is this going to be over? How much longer? There's supposed to be a sketch show in this venue about guys playing with their testicles after this!*

FAILING UPWARD

I'll chalk it up to good agenting that Marc Provissiero, our agent, was able to parlay *Matt & Ben* into a pilot deal. Marc was passionate, young, and did charming things like disappear to Costa Rica and send us bottles of hot sauce in the mail. He could also switch from making small talk to becoming fiercely intense about our careers, making unwavering eye contact with his blue eyes. He's the kind of guy you could see successfully carrying off an Aaron Sorkin monologue in real life. If he ever quits show business he could be a leader of a successful cult. It goes without saying he was a killer agent.

Our pilot, based on our lives in Brooklyn, was set up at a network that no longer exists, which I will call SHT. It was called *Mindy & Brenda*. It was supposed to be *Laverne & Shirley* but sexier, I guess. Or like *Mork & Mindy,* replacing the alien character with Brenda as a sensible earthling.

We had a group of producers for the project, a few of whom I still think of with great affection. One was the legendary Tom Werner, who produced *The Cosby Show* and *Roseanne.* Tom would mention offhandedly that he'd caught a great baseball game the night before, and we'd later realize he was talking about sitting in his box at Fenway Park watching the Boston Red Sox, the Major League Baseball team he owned. I liked Tom a lot because he never got flustered or anxious, ever. We could burst into his office with Nancy Grace–level anger over a network note, and Tom would sit back in his chair and distract us with a great anecdote about Bill Cosby. He was our wise, tan, and detached uncle.

When we wrote the show, we assumed that we would be playing the parts of Mindy and Brenda. This turned out to be a misguided assumption, because SHT had no intention of ever allowing that. We were told we would have to audition for the parts of Mindy and Brenda. *Mindy* and *Brenda*. I don't know why we were surprised. SHT at this time was a network known largely for casting models to act in television programs and hoping audiences would enjoy good-looking people saying lines they had learned phonetically. If I sound bitter, it's because I am still a little bitter. Who wouldn't be?

If you were ever considering sitting in a room with a group of actresses who bear a passing resemblance to you but are much, much thinner and more conventionally attractive, don't do it. You might think it has value as an anthropological exercise but it doesn't. I was sitting in an audition room with a bunch of girls who were the "after" picture to my "before." My audition for *Bombay Dreams* was Christmas morning compared to this. This was how I found out that I could convincingly play Ben Affleck but not Mindy Kaling.

The network cast two stunningly pretty and perfectly sweet actresses. By the time we shot the pilot, though, the script made little sense. It had suffered from the daily changes made by SHT execs who put too much stock in "what is cool now?" Being "zeitgeisty" was the biggest criterion for the show. Being funny as maybe fifth important, after wardrobe choices, hair styling, cross-promotional opportunities with advertisers, and edgy sound effects. By the time we shot the script, *Mindy & Brenda* bore no resemblance to us, figuratively or literally. I believe in the shooting draft they were both fashion bloggers who worked at a cupcake bakery and were constantly referring to their iPods. (This was 2004, when iPods were the white-hot reference.) I'm not proud of that script.

The pilot didn't get picked up, my agents were disappointed, and I was very, very happy. I'd had so little Hollywood experience that I wasn't smart enough to know that this was a big career setback. I was just relieved that that show wouldn't go forward with my name on it. The only other thing I had keeping me in Los Angeles was that I'd been hired as a staff writer for six episodes of a mid-season NBC show that was the remake of a British show called *The Office.**

---

* Notice how I laid in all that dramatic irony here? Like in *Titanic*, when Kate Winslet's character loved those weird paintings by a little-known artist named Picasso? And in the audience of the theater you were laughing to yourself because you knew Picasso turned out to be kind of a big deal? I'm trying to tell you that I'm Picasso.

Hollywood: My Good Friend Who Is Also a Little Embarrassing

Types of Women in Romantic Comedies
Who Are Not Real

WHEN I WAS a kid, Christmas vacation meant renting VHS copies of romantic comedies from Blockbuster and watching them with my parents at home. *Sleepless in Seattle* was big, and so was *When Harry Met Sally*. I laughed along with everyone else at the scene where Meg Ryan fakes an orgasm at the restaurant without even knowing what an orgasm was. In my mind, she was just being kind of loud and silly at a diner, and that was hilarious enough for me.

I love romantic comedies. I feel almost sheepish writing that, because the genre has been so degraded in the past twenty years or so that admitting you like these movies is essentially an admission of mild stupidity. But that has not stopped me from watching them.

I enjoy watching people fall in love on-screen so much that I can suspend my disbelief for the contrived situations that only happen in the heightened world of romantic comedies. I have come to enjoy the moment when the normal lead guy, say, slips and falls right on top of the hideously expensive wedding cake. I actually feel robbed when the female lead's dress *doesn't* get torn open at a baseball game while the JumboTron is on her. I simply regard romantic comedies as a subgenre of sci-fi, in which the world created therein has different rules than my regular human world. Then I just lap it up. There is no difference between Ripley from *Alien* and any Katherine Heigl character. They're all participating in the same level of made-up awesomeness, and I enjoy every second of it.

So it makes sense that in this world there are many specimens of women who I do not think exist in real life, like Vulcans or UFO people or whatever. They are:

THE KLUTZ

When a beautiful actress is in a movie, executives wrack their brains to find some kind of flaw in her that still allows her to be palatable. She can't be overweight or not perfect-looking, because who would want to see that? A not 100-percent-perfect-looking-in-every-way female? You might as well film a dead squid decaying on a beach somewhere for two hours.

So they make her a Klutz.

The 100-percent-perfect-looking female is perfect in every way, except that she constantly falls down. She bonks her head on things. She trips and falls and spills soup on her affable date. (Josh Lucas. Is that his name? I know it's two first names. Josh George? Brad Mike? Fred Tom? Yes, it's Fred Tom.) Our Klutz clangs into Stop signs while riding a bike, and knocks over giant displays of expensive fine china. Despite being five foot nine and weighing 110 pounds, she is basically like a drunk buffalo who has never been a part of human society. But Fred Tom loves her anyway.

THE ETHEREAL WEIRDO

The smart and funny writer Nathan Rabin coined the term *Manic Pixie Dream Girl* to describe a version of this archetype after seeing Kirsten Dunst in the movie *Elizabethtown*. This girl can't be pinned down and may or may not show up when you make concrete plans. She wears gauzy blouses and braids. She decides to dance in the rain and weeps uncontrollably if she sees a sign for a missing dog or cat. She spins a globe, places her finger on a random spot, and decides to move there. This ethereal weirdo abounds in movies, but nowhere else. If she were from real life, people would think she was a homeless woman and would cross the street to avoid her, but she is essential to the male fantasy that even if a guy is boring, he deserves a woman who will find him fascinating and pull him out of himself by forcing him to go skinny-dipping in a stranger's pool.

THE WOMAN WHO IS OBSESSED WITH HER CAREER AND IS NO FUN AT ALL

I, Mindy Kaling, basically have two full-time jobs. I regularly work sixteen hours a day. But like most of the other people I know who are similarly busy, I think I'm a pleasant, pretty normal person. I am slightly offended by the way busy working women my age are presented in film. I'm not, like, always barking orders into my hands-free phone device and telling people constantly, "I have no time for this!" I didn't completely forget how to be nice or feminine because I have a career. Also, since when does having a job necessitate women having their hair pulled back in a severe, tight bun? Often this uptight woman has to "re-learn" how to seduce a man because her estrogen leaked out of her from leading so many board meetings, and she has to do all sorts of crazy, unnecessary crap, like eat a hot dog in a libidinous way or something. Having a challenging job in movies means the compassionate, warm, or sexy side of your brain has fallen out.

THE FORTY-TWO-YEAR-OLD MOTHER OF THE THIRTY-YEAR-OLD MALE LEAD

I am so accustomed to the young mom phenomenon, that when I saw the poster for *The Proposal* I wondered for a second if the proposal in the movie was Ryan Reynolds suggesting he send his mother, Sandra Bullock, to an old-age home.

However, given the popularity of teen moms right now, this could actually be the wave of the future.

THE SASSY BEST FRIEND

You know that really horny and hilarious best friend who is always asking about your relationship and has nothing really going on in her own life? She always wants to meet you in coffee shops or wants to go to Bloomingdale's to sample perfumes? She runs a chic dildo store in the West Village? Nope? Okay, that's this person.

THE SKINNY WOMAN WHO IS BEAUTIFUL AND TONED BUT ALSO GLUTTONOUS AND DISGUSTING

Again, I am more than willing to suspend my disbelief during a romantic comedy for good set decoration alone. One pristine kitchen from a Nancy Meyers movie like in *It's Complicated* is worth five Diane Keatons being caught half-clad in a topiary or whatever situation her character has found herself in.

But sometimes even my suspended disbelief isn't enough. I am speaking of the gorgeous and skinny heroine who is also a disgusting pig when it comes to food. And everyone in the movie—her parents, her friends, her boss—are all complicit in this huge lie. They are constantly telling her to stop eating and being such a glutton. And this actress, this poor skinny actress who so clearly lost weight to play the likable lead, has to say things like "Shut up you guys! I love cheesecake! If I want to eat an entire cheesecake, I will!" If you look closely, you can see this woman's ribs through the dress she's wearing—that's how skinny she is, this cheesecake-loving cow.

You wonder, as you sit and watch this movie, what the characters would do if they were confronted by an actual average American woman. They would all kill themselves, which would actually be kind of an interesting movie.

THE WOMAN WHO WORKS IN AN ART GALLERY

How many freakin' art galleries are out there? Are people constantly buying visual art or something? This posh-smart-classy job is a favorite in movies. It's in the same realm as kindergarten teacher in terms of accessibility: guys don't really get it, but the trappings of it are likable and nonthreatening.

> ART GALLERY WOMAN: Dust off the Rothko. We have an important buyer coming into town and this is a really big deal for my career. I have no time for this!

This is one of the rare clichés that actually has a male counterpart. Whenever you meet a handsome, charming, successful man in a romantic comedy, the heroine's friend always says the same thing. "He's really successful—he's an . . .
(say it with me)
. . . architect!"
There are like nine people in the entire world who are architects, and one of them is my dad. None of them looks like Patrick Dempsey.

All About *The Office*

*T*HE OFFICE is a big chapter in my life, so that is why it's a big chapter in my book. It is what I'm best known for and what people ask me about the most. I'd like to be cool enough to say I'm sick of talking about it, the way Jennifer Lopez doesn't want to talk about her butt anymore, but *The Office* is still a significant part of my life, and I think it is awesome. So, here we go.

People are always asking me what my castmates on *The Office* are really like: Is Steve Carell really as nice as he seems? Is John Krasinski as cool as Jim in real life? What about Rainn Wilson; is he as big an egomaniac as Dwight? The answers are: yes, yes, and much, much worse.

I love watching *The Real Housewives* of any city, so I have an appreciation for lunatic divas. So it is a little disappointing that there aren't any on our show. Sure, there are occasional tantrums and arguments, and as I've said, Rainn is the absolute worst, but other than that, there's not too much to tell. We don't have any sensational meltdowns if, say, Catering accidentally puts chickpeas in a star's salad. Actually, wait, maybe *I'm* that person. I will throw a salad across the room if there are chickpeas in it, I swear to God.

Because people on the set are so normal, I'm usually very happy to dish about them. But I walk away from these encounters slightly disturbed, because I realize: no one wonders what I'm like in real life, because they assume I am Kelly Kapoor.

Obviously, this confusion is not something I would mind if I were playing Lara Croft or a Supreme Court justice or Serena Williams or something, but when you're playing a bit of a self-ish, boy-crazy narcissist, it's a concern. And even though I'm a writer and producer (and sometimes director, technically making me a quadruple threat, what of it?) of the series, people tend to forget this in the face of the fact that the character Kelly and I both love shopping. To clear things up, here is a list of some differences between us, as I see it.

Things Kelly Would Do That I Would Not
- Fake a pregnancy for attention
- Fake a rape for attention
- Text while showering
- Consider driving away from the site of a vehicular manslaughter
- Plant evidence of cheating in order to confront a boyfriend
- Cry about a celebrity breakup
- Write a letter of support to Jennifer Aniston
- Write a mean anonymous letter to Lance Armstrong re: Sheryl Crow
- Use a voodoo doll
- Create an online persona to cyberbully a girl into being anorexic
- Blackmail a boyfriend into taking her out to dinner

Things Kelly and I Would Both Do
- Choreograph and star in a music video
- Fake our own deaths to catch a serial killer
- Cry at work occasionally
- Memorize our credit card numbers to shop online with ease

· Drive with our parking brake on
· Go to goop.com every day
· Spend hours following a difficult recipe, hate the way it tastes, and throw it out to go to McDonald's
· Get upset if we're not invited to a party
· Go on trendy and slightly dangerous diets
· Hold a royal wedding viewing party

Some of the world's best comedians successfully play versions of themselves, like Woody Allen, Tina Fey, Ray Romano, and Larry David, but I am not doing that with Kelly. You'll all get to see me ingeniously playing a version of myself when I do my own show, *Mindy Kaling: Escaped War Criminal Hunter*. Flying to Bolivia to extradite or execute Nazis? That is so quintessentially *me*.

I have the opportunity to write for Kelly, but more often than not, I am not really able to. When you write an episode of *The Office*, you are required to be on set supervising the shooting of your episode. If I'm acting as Kelly, that means I can't be supervising the set as a producer, because I'm too busy acting in a scene, and so I have less control over the overall quality of the episode. Believe me, I'd love for Kelly to be in the show more, slowly encroaching on the leads' air time until the show is renamed *My Name is Kelly* or *A-B-C-D-E-F-G-H-I-J-KELLY!* But given how many characters we have, the tertiary characters like Kelly tend to have one or two great lines per episode. Wait, what's the thing that comes after tertiary? That's Kelly.

LONG PAUSES WITH GREG DANIELS, GETTING HIRED, AND THE FIRST SEASON

People ask me all the time how I got hired onto *The Office*. Another common question is how do I manage to stay so down-

John Krasinski and I, professional actors,
unable to complete a scene without laughing.

to-earth in the face of such incredible success? This I can't explain. It probably has something to do with innate goodness or something. A third frequently asked question is: "Girl, where you from? Trinidad? Guyana? Dominican Republic? You married? You got kids?" This is mostly asked by guys on the sidewalk selling I LOVE NEW YORK paraphernalia in New York City.

My career in Hollywood is owed to a man named Greg Daniels. He and his wife, Susanne, saw *Matt & Ben,* and soon after, I got a call from my agent, Marc, who told me that Greg wanted to meet me for a general.

General is short for "general meeting," which is one of the most vague and dreaded Hollywood inventions. It essentially means "I am curious about you, but I don't want to have a meal with you, and I want there to be little expectation of any tangible outcome from our meeting." Most of the time with generals, neither person knows exactly why they are meeting the other person, and so you talk about L.A. traffic patterns and which celebrities are looking too thin these days. The meetings are fun if you like chatting, which I do, but frustrating if you like moving forward with your life, which I also do. But usually you get a free bottle of water.

I was incredibly nervous meeting Greg, because his reputation preceded him. Even my dad knew who he was, because of the opening credits in *King of the Hill,* one of the only animated shows he didn't think was destroying the minds of American youth. Greg had been on the staff of *The Harvard Lampoon,* a writer for *Saturday Night Live* (where he was writing partners with Conan O'Brien), *The Simpsons,* and *Seinfeld,* and created *King of the Hill.* If he'd died after just doing that, people still would have been sad to read his obituary. When I met him, he had just turned forty.

I got to the meeting early. It was held at the *King of the Hill* offices in Century City. Century City is a commercial business area with lots of gleaming high-rises. To help you visualize it, this is the area where Alan Rickman held all those people hostage in *Die Hard.* A bored twentysomething guy greeted me at Reception. Actually, he did not greet me. It took him a full minute or so before he looked away from his computer game to acknowledge me standing nervously in front of his desk. When people show a lack of excitement to see me, I compensate by complimenting the hell out of them. It always exacerbates the problem, but I cannot stop. I focused on his tidy work area.

ME: What a clean desk. If it were mine it'd be a disaster, ha ha.

RECEPTIONIST GUY: This isn't my desk. They moved me here when the season ended. I literally have nothing to do with this desk.

We stared at each other for a few moments, until he told me to sit down next to a full-size cutout of Peggy Hill.

Marc had warned me that Greg was "a little quiet and pensive," but no one could have warned me just how quiet and pensive. Greg is the frequent perpetrator of crazy-long pauses in conversation. Like, minutes long. My meeting with him was about two and a half hours, but if you transcribed it, it would have had the content of a fifteen-minute conversation. Greg would reference all kinds of books and articles, and instead of paraphrasing them, like any normal lazy person, he'd insist on going online and finding the exact line or quote from the secondary source, adding another five-minute silent section to the meeting, during which he wordlessly surfed online. Later I would realize this is Greg's signature style. He likes to take in people past the point where they can be putting on a show to impress him. Or, this is my interpretation. He might just have been zoning out and forgot I was there.

Greg's a very low-key guy, with the bearing of a gentle, athletic scientist. We talked about New Hampshire, our dads, books, and elaborate Indian weddings. It was fun, and I unexpectedly learned a lot. I remember leaving the meeting with a few print-outs; one was MapQuest directions to a diner Greg loved eating at, called John O'Groats, and the other was an article about the history of the architecturally interesting library where Greg went to high school.

Now, I should give some context of that year in television. NBC had high hopes for three comedies that year: *Committed*, a show about eccentric friends living together in New York City; an animated show, *Father of the Pride*; and *Joey*, the spin-off of *Friends*. I could not get meetings with any of these hot shows. Like, not even close. Marc hustled and got me a meeting with only one other show, *Nevermind Nirvana*, a pilot about an interracial married couple. I drove to Burbank to meet with the executives. While I was sitting in the waiting area, the producer got a call: the show had not gotten picked up. The receptionist informed me of the news, and immediately started packing her stuff up in a box. I validated my parking and left. I literally didn't even make it into the room. So, technically, meeting Greg was my first and only staffing meeting in my career.

A week or so later, Marc called and told me Greg wanted to hire me as a staff writer for season one of *The Office*. Before I could get too excited, he let me know I had been hired for six episodes for a show that was premiering mid-season. This was the smallest amount of contracted work you could do and still qualify for Writers Guild membership. I didn't care. I was a television writer! With health insurance!

Friendless, I celebrated the best way I could. I went straight to Canter's Deli, sat in a booth, and ordered a huge frosty Coke and a sandwich called the Brooklyn Ave. (a less healthy version of a Reuben, if that is possible), and gabbed with my best friends and mom on the phone for two hours. An elderly man who was eating with his wife at a nearby table came over to my booth. "You're being very loud and rude," he said. "Your voice is so high-pitched and piercing."

I started work in July. At that time, I lived alone in a small, damp apartment I found on Fairfax Avenue and Fountain Boulevard, which I did not know was the nexus of all of transvestite social life in West Hollywood. I did not even have the basic L.A. savvy to ask my landlord for a parking space, so I parked blocks away from my house and enjoyed late-night interactions with strangely tall, flat-chested women named Felice or Vivica, who always wanted rides to the Valley. If my life at the time had been a sitcom, an inebriated tranny gurgling "Heeeeey, giiiirrrrrll!" would have been my "Norm!"

A giant billboard for a gay sex chat line was twenty feet from my apartment door. You have to understand, this was before I became the international and fabulous gay icon that I am today, so it made me uncomfortable. (Now I'm basically Lady Gaga and Gavin Newsom times a million.) When my parents came to visit me, I would try to distract them from seeing it by pointing across the street to a Russian produce market, which I was 70 percent sure was a front for a crime consortium. "Isn't that cool, Mom and Dad? I can get my produce locally."

My parents visited a lot. It was a lonely time. I started to look forward to my encounters with Felice and Vivica. "Heeeyyy, Curry Spice! Heeey, Giiiirrrrll!"

But mostly, I just wanted to start work.

Being a staff writer was very stressful. I knew I was a funny person, but I was so inexperienced in this atmosphere. Joking around with Brenda and writing plays on the floor of our living room in Brooklyn was intimate and safe, and entwined in our friendship. But I wasn't friends with these guys. I was the only staff writer on the show (the others outranked me) and had never been in a writers' room. Most of the stress came, honestly, because the other writers were so experienced and funny and I was worried I couldn't keep up. I was scared Greg would notice this inequity of talent and that he'd fire me in a two-hour, pause-laden meeting. I dreaded the pauses more than the firing.

The full-time writers for season one were Greg, Paul Lieberstein, Mike Schur, B. J. Novak, and me. Larry Wilmore and Lester Lewis were consultants, which meant they wrote three of the five days of the week. For some reason I thought Greg, B.J., and Mike were all best friends, because they had all gone to Harvard and been on *The Harvard Lampoon* (even though their times at Harvard didn't even overlap). I'll never forget one day at lunch, when Mike asked B.J. to go to a Red Sox–Dodgers game, while I stewed angrily on the other side of the room, feeling left out.

"I'll get you, you clique-y sons of bitches," I thought.

You know what? I never did get them. I'm just realizing now. I should totally still get them.

But as is the case with most people you are stuck with for many hours, they slowly became my good friends. The job of comedy writer is essentially to sit and have funny conversations about hypothetical situations, and you are rewarded for originality of detail. It is exhilarating, and I didn't want it to stop. I soon started dreading the weekends, because weekends meant saying good-bye to this creative, cheerful atmosphere.

I will always remember *Chappelle's Show* very fondly because besides being one of the funniest shows ever, it served as my good friend at the time. I'd watch every episode, and then watch them again later that day to hear the jokes again. Sometimes on a Saturday night I would fall asleep watching it on my sofa, like Dave Chappelle and I were best friends chatting until we fell asleep. I was twenty-four.

I did not know at the time that this year with Greg, Paul, B.J., and Mike would be where I essentially learned how to write comedy. This small group wrote the first six episodes of that first season of *The Office*. They were, and are, four of my favorite people in the world. They are also the four funniest people I know. I have fought bitterly with them, too—I mean real fights, knock-down-drag-outs—which I'll rationalize to mean they are my true friends. I won't say anymore about them, because none of them are lacking in confidence, and honestly, they're like three compliments away from becoming monsters.

WRITER FIGHTS, OR DON'T FIGHT WITH GREG DANIELS!

Writer fights are always exciting and traumatic, and I get into them all the time. I am a confident writer, a hothead, and have a very thin skin for any criticism. This charming combination of personality traits makes me an argument machine on our staff. A halfway compliment my friend and *The Office* showrunner Paul Lieberstein once paid me was that "it's a good thing you turn in good drafts, because you are impossible to rewrite." Thanks

Paul! All I heard was "Mindy, you're the best writer we've ever had. I cherish you. We all do."

This was taken between takes of "The Dundies," the season two premiere, which I wrote. We shot from dawn until late at night in a former Chili's restaurant in the deep San Fernando Valley. I am taking a ladylike nap on the floor while Paul Lieberstein writes notes on a script.

I tend to fight with Greg the most. My friend and fellow *Office* writer Steve Hely believes it is because I am emotional and intuitive and Greg is more cerebral and logical. Or, as I think of it, I am a sensitive poet and Greg is a mean robot. Our fighting is legendary. One time, late at night, our script coordinator, Sean, and our head writer, Danny, both brought in their dogs, and upon seeing each other, they got into a violent, barking fight. Paul Lieberstein glanced over and joked, "Oh, I thought that was Greg and Mindy."

What do we fight about? I wish I could say they were big, smart, philosophical issues about writing or comedy, but sometimes they're as small as "If we do that cold open where Kevin dumps a tureen of chili on himself, I will quit this show." We did that cold open, by the way, and it was a hit, and I'm still working at the show. I can get a little theatrical. Which makes sense, because, after all, I came up through the *theater* (said in my snootiest *Masterpiece Theatre* voice).

I will tell you about the worst fight we ever had. In a particularly heated rewrite session for the season-three episode "Grief Counseling," I was arguing with Greg so much, he finally said, in front of all twelve writers, "If you're going to resist what I'm doing here, you can just go home, Mindy."

Greg never sends anyone home, or even hints at it. Greg is the kind of guy who is so agreeable I frequently find him on our studio lot embroiled in some long conversation with a random person while his lunch is getting cold in his to-go container. And he's the boss. I would never talk to anyone if I were boss. I would only talk to my attorney and my psychic. So, anyway, my very nice boss had just hugely reprimanded me. Greg suggesting I go home unless I adjusted my attitude was the harshest he'd ever been to anyone in the three years I'd been on the show. There was silence. No one looked at me. People pretended to be absorbed in their phones. One writer didn't even have a phone, so he just pretended to be absorbed in his hand.

I was so embarrassed and angry I got up, stomped out the room, stole a twenty-four-pack of bottled water from the production office, kicked the bumper of Greg's car, and left the studio.

This is what I get for trying to make the show better? I'm funnier and a better writer than every single one of those assholes, I thought, angrily. I pictured myself accepting the Mark Twain Prize for American Humor at the Kennedy Center, and all those other writers watching from home, with the hope that I might acknowledge them, and I pointedly wouldn't. Instead, I'd thank Thalia, the Greek muse of comedy. I'd freaking thank *Thalia* over those guys. I drove to a nail salon in a mini-mall a mile away and angrily sat down for a manicure.

"Señora has the day off?" the woman soaking my nails asked me, congenially.

"Nope! I got kicked out of work!" I replied. She stopped what she was doing.

"Oh, you fired?" she asked, concerned.

Hearing her say "fired" sent a spiky shudder down my spine. I looked at my soaking cuticles. I saw the soft hands of a babied comedy writer who had never known a hard day's work. Did I really want to be unemployed? Did I want to jeopardize this amazing job I had dreamed about having since I was thirteen? Did I really want to be a receptionist at my mother's ob/gyn office, where I would need to learn Spanish?

I immediately stood up, dried my hands, handed some cash to the puzzled woman, and raced back to work. I quietly entered the writers' room and sat down.

My friend and fellow writer Lee Eisenberg looked at me quizzically and texted: WHERE HAVE YOU BEEN?

I texted back: THE BATHROOM.

Greg did not acknowledge my absence, or find out that I'd kicked his car, and it blew over. The bottles of water remained mine, bwah ha ha! That evening, when I had my nightly chat with my mother on the way home from work, I made the mistake of telling her about what had happened. I was hoping to get consoled for a bad day at work. Instead she yelled at me. "Are you crazy? You owe everything to Greg Daniels!" Mom always says "Greg Daniels," as though there were a few people at work with the first name Greg and I might not know who she was talking about. (There aren't.) "Greg Daniels took a chance on you and changed your life! Don't fight with Greg Daniels!" Dad got on the phone from the upstairs line, as he always does.

He agreed with Mom. "I know you get upset, Min. But you have to be professional." I am still trying to follow this terrific advice, only somewhat successfully, five years later.

The season six writers and editors.

STEVE CARELL IS NICE BUT IT IS SCARY

It has been said many times, but it is true: Steve Carell is a very nice guy. His niceness manifests itself mostly in the fact that he never complains. You could screw up a handful of takes outside in 104-degree smog-choked Panorama City heat, and Steve Carell's final words before collapsing of heat stroke would be a friendly and hopeful "Hey, you think you have that shot yet?"

I've always found Steve gentlemanly and private, like a Jane Austen character. The one notable thing about Steve's niceness is that he is also very smart, and that kind of niceness has always made me nervous. When smart people are nice, it's always terrifying, because I know they're taking in everything and thinking all kinds of smart and potentially judgmental things. Steve could never be as funny as he is, or as darkly observational an actor, without having an extremely acute sense of human flaws. As a result, I'm always trying to impress him, in the hope that he'll go home and tell his wife, Nancy, "Mindy was so funny and cool on set today. She just gets it."

Getting Steve to talk shit was one of the most difficult seven-year challenges, but I was determined to do it. A circle of actors could be in a fun, excoriating conversation about, say, Dominique Strauss-Kahn, and you'd shoot Steve an encouraging look that said, "Hey, come over here; we've made a space for you! We're trashing Dominique Strauss-Kahn to build cast rapport!" and the best he might offer is "Wow. If all they say about him is true, that is nuts," and then politely excuse himself to go to his trailer. That's it. That's all you'd get. Can you believe that? He just would not engage. That is some willpower there. I, on the other hand, hear someone briefly mentioning Rainn, and I'll immediately launch into "Oh my god, Rainn's so horrible." But Carell is just one of those infuriating, classy Jane Austen guys.

Later I would privately theorize that he never involved himself in gossip because—and I am 99 percent sure of this—he is secretly Perez Hilton.

WHERE I WORK

Many people assume *The Office* is shot in Scranton, Pennsylvania, because we take pains to shoot on locations that are green and East Coast–looking. Other people think we shoot on a picturesque studio lot like you see on the tour of Universal Studios, where Jaws is swimming happily near the *Desperate Housewives* cul-de-sac and down the block from an immolating car from the *Backdraft* set. Not so.

Anyone who comes to visit the set of *The Office* always says the

Rainn Wilson, violent ogre.

same thing when they leave: "Holy crap, that was scary!" This is because we shoot at the end of a dead-end street on an industrial block of Panorama City, in the San Fernando Valley, which sounds great—who doesn't love panoramas? But don't be fooled! The name is a trick. At one point Panorama City was part of Van Nuys, but Van Nuys did whatever the opposite of secede is to it. Expelled it? I'll put it this way. Van Nuys took one look at Panorama City and was like, "Uh, get your own name. We don't want to have anything to do with you."

We're at the end of a block with a gun parts warehouse, a neon sign store, and a junkyard. Our street is also a favored drag-racing strip for competitive, bored Mexican teenagers. We're always having to stop filming and wait for the noise to die down from junkyard dogs barking and gun parts being drilled. Come to think of it, there might actually be an immolating car around here once in a while. Take that, Universal Studios!

I love our set because we are isolated from other shows. Isolation is good, because there are no distractions to the work, and believe me, I get distracted easily. There is no cool shopping or dining or anything near us whatsoever, so we can only focus on working on the show. It makes us feel sequestered and secluded, which I think is good for creativity. Also, I can run out at any time and buy my gun parts.

KELLY KAPOOR GETS GIFT BAGS

When I started attending events associated with *The Office,* I started to receive gift bags. I'd recall breathless accounts from magazines of gifts like sapphire earrings, lifetime memberships to fancy gyms, gift certificates for total facial reconstruction plastic surgery, week-long stays at wildlife reserves where you get to touch the lions, and $500 jars of miracle face cream made from human placenta. It seemed like the greatest racket ever, and in 2006, I started to participate in it.

The way it works is you go to an awards show for which you've spent a crazy amount of money getting dressed up. After you win or lose in your categories, there is a nontelevised portion of the evening where you and every other person at the event gets herded into a giant windowless room and fed a hot buffet of food on par with a medium-fancy bar mitzvah. The thing is the food tastes insanely good because you've not eaten anything all day. After mingling for a little while, and mentally ranking the gowns of the other actresses so you can call your mom and give her the scoop, you trade in a parking ticket–like stub to some stressed-out looking woman at the exit and she gives you a black canvas bag packed with goodies. You get really excited. And then you open it up.

What I Have Gotten in My Gift Bags Over the Years
- protein bars
- a personal hygiene spray that I can only describe as a butt freshener

- socks with individual toes
- a travel-size tube of toothpaste for "women's teeth"
- a *SpongeBob SquarePants* keychain
- a mechanical pencil (kinda cool, but it was instantly stolen when I took it to work)
- weird coffee pods that work only if you buy the coffee machine that the pods are made for
- tan silicone cutlets you glue to your real breasts
- a crotchless girdle meant to hold your back fat in
- a children's book written by a lead in the original *Beverly Hills 90210*
- a diabetes cookbook (I actually love this)

The gift bags are junk bags. I'm not telling you this to complain, but rather to relieve you of any romantic notions you might have of them. Use those romantic notions for something else, like thinking about the significance and grandeur of our National Mint. Not only would you never purchase any of the stuff in these gift bags, but you would not even give it to a relative you have a chilly relationship with. There is, however, one excellent perk we get on our show: I've enjoyed an endless supply of free paper, paperclips, envelopes, and office supplies since joining *The Office,* because I steal props on a regular basis.

BECOMING A LITTLE BIT FAMOUS

When you have it as good as I know I do, work-wise, you rarely have time to enjoy your fabulous good fortune, because you're too busy worrying about when it will run out. After the first season of *The Office,* I remember Jenna Fischer, Angela Kinsey, and I got turned away from a party thrown by a famous magazine at a fancy hotel on Sunset Boulevard. The party coordinators didn't think being on *The Office* warranted our getting in. We stood and watched the *One Tree Hill* cast waltz in with no problem. The PR people at the party regarded us with the disdain normally reserved for on-set tutors for child actors. (For the record, there is usually no one weirder on a set than the tutor for child actors. They tend to be aging hippie ladies with inappropriately long hair tied coquettishly in a messy gray braid, and an all-denim outfit that would put Jay Leno to shame.)

Luckily, I was not in the aging child-tutor stage for long, though. Midway through season two, we were finally getting recognition due to our track record of a dozen great episodes, and people were into us. It was glorious. The highlight was one Saturday, when I was vacuuming my car at a gas station on Santa Monica Boulevard during the Gay Pride parade and a group of gay veterans in uniform shrieked, "Oh my God, it's Kelly Kapoor!" The guys at the gas station thought I was hot shit.

Being the "It" show in season two presented its own challenges, though. A common refrain we heard was "I disliked your

This is a photo of when I directed "Michael's Last Dundies," which I also wrote. In this moment I am explaining what comedy is to Will Ferrell.

first season, but by the second season you really came into your own." I think people thought their compliment meant more if they tempered it with something insulting first. As if I were to say, "I initially thought you were ugly, but then you walked closer to me and I realized you were pretty." I love our first season. I think it is a little dark and really funny. I found the phrase "came into your own" especially weird, as though *The Office* finally developed breasts or something.

WHAT WE HAVE TO BE SCARED ABOUT

What's coming up next is a perennial fear in the television world. Some people who work in the industry confidently ignore all new good shows, saying, "There's room for lots of good television. That won't affect us," but that's simply not true. There's room for a little good scripted television and many, many reality TV shows about monitored weight loss. If the science were there to genetically clone Jillian Michaels, our network would just be different filmed iterations of obese people losing weight, all day long. My friend Charlie Grandy once joked that it is only a matter of time before there is a category at the Emmys for "Best Extreme Weight Loss Program."

In the spring, when the networks trot out their lineup of new shows, you may idly think, Meh, maybe I'll try this one or DVR that one, but I get a little paranoid trying to figure out whether any newcomer is going to beat us into a painful death by primetime scheduling. I've made a list of potential shows that I believe would kill *The Office* in the ratings:

- *I Want to Be Able to Walk for My Wedding!*: Jillian Michaels helps a morbidly obese couple confined to their sofa lose weight for their nuptials.
- *I Want to Be Able to Walk When I Officiate a Wedding!*: Jillian Mi-

chaels helps an obese priest, confined to his parish, officiate a wedding.

- *Obese Priest:* A priest who eats too much dessert helps a group of at-risk, but hilarious teens.
- *Sing-Sing-Sings!:* A singing competition in Sing Sing prison.
- *The Weekly Hangover:* A reality show where three friends are chloroformed and put in a random dangerous situation, like in the movie *The Hangover,* and have to piece back what happened to their lives.
- *Interspecies Friendships:* Have you ever seen that YouTube video where the elephant is friends with the collie? Or the one where the turtle and the hippopotamus are best friends? I could watch those for hours. These are the buddy comedies people crave.

I actually think I might create *Interspecies Friendships.* A smart, small observational show about two animals who are friends against all odds. It'll be a tough sell at first, but by season two it'll really come into its own. But it'll never be as good as the original British version, *Interspecies Chums.*

Franchises I Would Like to Reboot

BY NOW YOU'VE seen what a savvy Hollywood person I am and wonder when I will be making my big jump from television to film. Here's where I explain everything and tell about some of my most exciting film projects in the pipeline.

Nobody likes it when Hollywood reboots beloved franchises. When I was hired to write for the NBC remake of the classic BBC show *The Office,* everyone had the immediate physical reaction of being around someone who had just farted.

The thing is at least we were trying to remake something that was excellent. What I have never understood is the rebooting of already terrible things. For example, take *The Dukes of Hazzard.* This was a show whose two greatest claims to fame were (a) a car that consistently jumped over large objects at critical moments, and (b) introducing Americans to the Daisy Duke short-shorts, which single-handedly lowered the average age of sexual intercourse in this country by several years. I loved the show as a four-year-old, but even then I kind of knew *The Dukes of Hazzard* was for kids. I thought, *This is good for me, or a five-year-old, tops.* So, when it got remade as a movie, I didn't quite understand.

But then I heard how much money it made and I thought, I need to get in on this, pronto. Here are some franchises I would like to reboot, for the love of the franchise and a little bit for the love of the money I think they would make.

A LEAGUE OF THEIR OWN

Unfortunately, a bit of an uphill battle here. As fun and frothy as this movie was, it was based on an actual historical event. The All-American Girls Professional Baseball League was a real thing. Also, I would reboot this movie only if I can play the Rosie O'Donnell part, and I'm pretty sure there weren't many Indian women in the United States in the 1940s.

THE HULK

I feel like if they're going to remake this every two or three years anyway, I want to get a shot at one.

OCEAN'S FIVE

Let's be real here. The first Ocean's film—not the 1960's *Ocean's 11;* how old do you think I am?—was great, but there were already four too many guys in it. Don Cheadle had, like, three lines in the entire movie. The films that came after *Ocean's Eleven,* where they kept adding people, were hard to follow. There were so many characters doing different Vegas-related missions. It made you feel like someone behind the scenes was out of control, like, oh my God, if we don't stop this person, all of the Screen Actors Guild is going to be in Danny Ocean's gang. That's why we need to do a prequel and cut out the ragtaggiest of the ragtag bunch. We do that Benjamin Button backward-aging special effect magic on Clooney, and bam! We've got a summer blockbuster.

VAN HELSING

Why was this movie so bad? It had all the ingredients of a great movie. The subject material (handsome European professor annihilates vampires) is the stuff dreams are made of. Hugh was in prime Jackman when he played smoldering Van Helsing. The lovely Kate Beckinsale was there, too, as pale beautiful lady friend or whatever. Why wasn't this a killer movie and a classic? I could so redo this, with the same cast, and make it a better movie. I'm throwing down the gauntlet, Van Helsing.

And speaking of movies about regular people destroying magical creatures:

GHOSTBUSTERS

I always wanted the reboot of *Ghostbusters* to be four girl-ghostbusters. Like, four normal, plucky women living in New York City searching for Mr. Right and trying to find jobs—but who also bust ghosts. I'm not an idiot, though. I know the demographic for *Ghostbusters* is teenage boys, and I know they would kill themselves if two ghostbusters had a makeover at Sephora. I just have always wanted to see a cool girl having her first kiss with a guy she's had a crush on, and then have to excuse herself to go trap the pissed-off ghosts of the Triangle Shirtwaist Factory fire or something. In my imagination, I am, of course, one of the ghostbusters, with the likes of say, Emily Blunt, Taraji Henson, and Natalie Portman. Even if I'm not the ringleader, I'm definitely the one who gets to say "I ain't afraid a no ghost." At least the first time.

Contributing Nothing
at *Saturday Night Live*

I WAS A dreadful guest writer on *Saturday Night Live*. Not like, destructively bad or anything, just a useless, friendly extra body in the *SNL* offices eating hamburgers for free, like Wimpy from *Popeye*.

I came into the show during the hiatus between seasons two and three of *The Office*. My friend Mike Schur, who had worked at *SNL* before *The Office*, recommended me to Mike Shoemaker, a producer over there. Mike Shoemaker and some others had liked an episode of *The Office* I'd written called "The Injury," where Michael grills his foot accidentally in a George Foreman Grill. Mike Shoemaker graciously invited me to write there for a few weeks. I later found out that most guest writers were there as a kind of "audition" for a permanent writing job, and they came prepared with lots of hilarious sketch ideas, even some partially written. But since I was coming straight from my *Office* job, I didn't have time to prepare, even if I had known I was supposed to.

I guess that's not entirely true. I was prepared in my own way, which is to say, I had packed several fashion-forward outfits that I bought from Nordstrom Rack with my mom, all of which were rendered useless immediately. Writers and actors at *SNL* looked cool but casual. When I heard of a "television writing job in New York City," I imagined a *Gossip Girl*–type aesthetic. My outfits of button-down shirts, an ironic broach, men's ties, kilts, and gold high-tops were completely stupid in the face of Seth Meyers's subtly awesome gray T-shirts and Levi's or whatever.

So, lesson one: fashion plays a relatively unimportant role in the day-to-day work life of *Saturday Night Live*. Okay, learned that.

Here's how the writing worked. The writers either wrote sketches alone or paired up with other people they collaborated with regularly. The problem is, I didn't know anyone, so I felt shy approaching anybody with ideas.

I shared a tiny windowless office with Kristen Wiig. This was, as you can imagine, incredibly exciting. We had no privacy, which was fine with me, because I was hoping the claustrophobic atmosphere of our shared office would be like a college dorm room, and that we'd become confidantes through our sheer physical proximity. It'd go down something like this:
(Joni Mitchell's *Blue* is playing on my computer.)

KRISTEN: God, I love this album.

ME: Me too. Doesn't it make you wish we'd been alive during Woodstock?

KRISTEN: Yes! I always think that when I listen to this!

ME: That's hilarious. Hey, do you want to go get some lunch and then hit Crabtree & Evelyn?

KRISTEN (as though I'm an idiot): Uhhh yeah. I mean if we can even fit out the door of this tiny office.

ME: You're so bad.

(We laugh and laugh.)

KRISTEN: Seriously, I wish we could've gone to Woodstock together.

This interaction didn't happen. As it turned out, Kristen Wiig was kind of busy at *Saturday Night Live*. She was almost never in our office. She was either rehearsing on set, at a fitting, or writing sketches with other people in their offices. It made sense, but it was disappointing.

At dinnertime, one Wednesday night, some production assistants brought out huge bags of food and put them on the main writers' conference room table. People trickled out of their offices to eat. I had spent the last four hours trying to write a sketch where Bill Hader was a pregnant female cat. I don't know why, but it seemed so funny to me at the time. Like so funny I would stop and look up at the ceiling thinking: "Oh man, this is gonna be so great when the others hear this aloud. Like 'Land Shark' for a new generation."

Among some of the writers were Amy Poehler, Seth Meyers, Rachel Dratch, and Tina Fey. It was a pretty awesome group, especially because a Tina sighting was rare back then, since she was editing her pilot (which was the pilot for *30 Rock*). While they all talked and goofed around, I sat at the table listening and smiling and saying nothing, like an upbeat foreign exchange student who spoke very little English.

The last time I had felt like that was when I was in ninth grade and I would have to wait after school in the eleventh-graders' student center for my brother to get his stuff so he could drive us home. I stood there smiling like an idiot, just excited to be in the presence of all these cool older people. "Stop smiling so much," my brother said to me once when he came to get me. "You look like a maniac."

I cowrote one bit that made it to air. It was a segment for Weekend Update where Chad Michael Murray was talking to Tina and Amy about why he needed to get married so much instead of just date women. Because even though he doesn't affect anyone in the slightest, I simply felt Chad Michael Murray needed to be satirized! Will Forte played the part valiantly. That might have been the most unnecessary little piece of comedy ever to grace *Saturday Night Live.* "Mom, Dad, I wrote a sketch for *SNL.* I'll explain who Chad Michael Murray is later."

My Bill Hader pregnant cat sketch got read at the table and went over so poorly I remember wondering if I should fake meningitis so that I could blame that for such a bad sketch. Or if I could, at all, play it off as so ironically terrible it was good. What? I'm not hipster enough for that? I started writing my agent an e-mail asking if I could leave after my first week there. I was literally in the middle of writing it when I heard a knock on my and Kristen's door. It was Amy Poehler.

ME: Hi. Kristen is on the stage, I think, but I can leave her a message.

AMY: Oh, I wanted to talk to you.

Amy went on to ask if I was going to go out with some of the writers and actors after work. I nodded yes, which was a huge lie. I had planned on sprinting back to the Sofitel (where they were putting me up a few blocks away) and falling asleep watching the syndicated *That '70s Show,* which I had done every night since I landed in New York. But Amy, being warm, prescient, Amy, said knowingly, "Why don't I just wait here for you and we can walk over together?"

Everyone has a moment when they discover they love Amy Poehler. For most people it happened sometime during her run on *Saturday Night Live.* For some it was when she came back to the show in 2009, nine months' pregnant, and did that complicated, hard-core Sarah Palin rap on Weekend Update.

I first noticed Amy when I was in high school and I saw her on Conan's first show. She was in a sketch playing Andy Richter's "little sister Stacey." Stacey had pigtails and headgear and was obsessed with Conan. As a performer, she was this pretty little gremlin, all elbows and blond hair and manic eyes. As a teenager, I tracked her career as best I could without the Internet, and was overjoyed when I saw she had become a cast member on *Saturday Night Live*. I loved when she played Kaitlin, with her cool stepdad, Rick.

But when this popular, pretty genius made this kind gesture to me? That's the moment I started adoring Amy Poehler. She knew I was going to be a coward, and she was going to have to gently facilitate me into being social. We walked over on Forty-ninth Street with a big group of people and Amy asked me about my life in L.A. I told her, super self-conscious about seeming nervous. This was the woman who, ten years earlier, had inspired me to keep my parents up until 1:00 a.m. to watch her on *Late Night with Conan O'Brien*. When I said something even a little bit funny, Amy cackled warmly. (This sounds weird, but that's the best way I know to describe Amy Poehler's laugh: a warm, intoxicating cackle.)

The evening that followed wasn't especially memorable. Many of her friends reasonably expected to talk to her, so I didn't get precious one-on-one Amy time. I had also forgotten to bring cash and had to borrow twenty dollars from a writer I barely knew. But I stayed the second week at *SNL*. Antonio Banderas was hosting, and at the read-through, I presented a new sketch. This hilarious sketch was about identical twins who were reunited when their parents died in the rubble when the Berlin Wall fell. After an almost laugh-free reading, Antonio looked over to his assistant, befuddled, and said, "Theese? Theese makes no sense to me."

All the humiliation was worth it for the one shining moment when Amy Poehler proposed we walk a few blocks together, late at night, in New York City in 2006.

Roasts Are Terrible

WITH THE EXCEPTION of organized dog fighting, or roller coasters named the Mind Eraser, there is no form of entertainment I like less than the modern-day televised roast.

It's a real shame, because I think creative, funny, even merciless teasing is one of the greatest cathartic ways to laugh and bring people together. This is, like, the point of wedding festivities, besides the drunk dancing to the Electric Slide.

I'm not going to rhapsodize about the Friars Club roasts of the 1960s, I promise. It's not like I'm yearning to return to some classy golden era of roasts, like those annoying people who only like entertainment from any time but the present. But what I do appreciate about old Friars Club roasts is that when, say, Freddie Prinze roasted Sammy Davis Jr., it seemed like (a) they actually knew each other, and (b) the people roasting weren't professional insulters. They had other careers, as comedians, actors, politicians. This was just something they did very well, from time to time. And it was affectionate.

When I see comedians roasting their victims, and viciously making light of their flaws, I want to put my hand on, say, David Hasselhoff's shoulder and say, "David, it gets better." If this isn't a hate crime, then what is? But mostly, I think of the roasters. Do they call up their parents excitedly, like, "Look, Ma! I made it! I'm eviscerating Pamela Anderson on television tonight for having STDs!" Jeff Ross is one of the most gifted living comedians, in my estimation, and he does roasts all the time, which is incredibly frustrating. Jeff's stand-up is truly funny, and it's much more relatable and observational than his roast material. He should have his own show where he's an awesome leading man. He should not be roasting cast members of *Jersey Shore*. Watching Jeff do roasts is like watching Andy Roddick destroy at Ping-Pong in your grandfather's basement.

I do not need to hear people tearing into Lisa Lampanelli for liking to have sex only with black men. I'm sad that this is her famous running gag. I'm sad that I now know this. I'm sad that a legitimate rung on the ladder of making it in comedy is writing hateful stuff about total strangers. I don't know. I also did not want to see photos of Osama Bin Laden's dead body. I think the two things are related.

When I watch roasts, I actually feel physically uncomfortable, like when I see a crow feast on a squirrel that has been hit by a car but has not stopped moving yet. The self-proclaimed no-holds-barred atmosphere reminds me of signs for strip clubs on Hollywood Boulevard: "We Have Crazy Girls. They Do Anything!" We don't have to do anything. Let's bar some holds.

My Favorite Eleven Moments in Comedy

WHEN I WAS a kid, I was obsessed with listing my favorite things. I kept an index card with all my favorite foods folded in my wallet, just in case anyone asked me what they were. Then when people walked away, I imagined they'd say: "Whoa, Mindy Kaling is so cool and self-actualized. McDonald's pancakes are her favorite food, and she was able to *tell me right away.*" I was prepared for all kinds of potential fun situations when I was kid. I kept a bathing suit in my backpack in case I went anywhere where there was a swimming pool. I grew up on the East Coast where pools are a really big deal, but still, I planned excessively.

When I started getting into comedy, my listing became even more important, because I thought having my favorite comedy moments on file said so much about me. I thought it'd be fun to share my favorites.

A disclaimer about these: they are all pretty recent, from the last ten or fifteen years. My boss Greg Daniels was appalled I had never heard of Jack Benny or Ernie Kovacs before I started working at *The Office.* I am sorry I'm not obsessed with *The Honeymooners* or *The Great Dictator,* or even *Caddyshack* or other classic comedy from the '60s, '70s, and '80s. This list is also pretty mainstream, so other comedy nerds will be mad I didn't include alternative comedy stuff. This list also doesn't include stand-up, because that would be its own can of excellent worms starring the likes of Louie C.K., Wanda Sykes, Mo'nique, Jerry Seinfeld, etc. I know there are probably glaring omissions. Come on guys. I'm not a professional list maker. Just be cool.

1. Will Ferrell Shouting from the Phone Booth in *Anchorman*

Anchorman is a strange little miracle of a movie, with some historic comedy film significance, too. It put together an all-star team of comedy actors that includes Will Ferrell, Paul Rudd, Steve Carell, and David Koechner. No other pairings of these guys would ever be as funny as this. I'm sure I'll go see, and really love, *Uncle Retreat* or whatever movie comes next, but it won't make my mouth drop like *Anchorman* did.

When Ron Burgundy—amazing names in this movie, by the way—believes his dog has been killed by an angry motorist (Jack Black, used perfectly), he is so overcome with grief, he can't do the news that night. He calls from a phone booth, in one of the funniest, most theatrical displays of grief I've ever seen. It's like grief with a capital G.

There's a heightened style of acting that Will Ferrell and Adam McKay employ in their movies that is incredibly difficult to pull off. If done poorly, heightened comedy acting can seem like you're watching an inadvertently campy kids' production of *12 Angry Men*. But it is Will Ferrell's sweet spot. He has made a career of making unlikely things not only totally work but also be the funniest things I've ever seen. (I'm of course referring to the movie *Elf*, whose premise reads like the ramblings of an insane little kid drunk off Christmas egg nog.)

2. Liz Lemon Crying Out of Her Mouth on *30 Rock*

Alec Baldwin's Jack Donaghy convinced Tina Fey's Liz Lemon to get eye surgery so she'll be more TV-friendly for her new talk show. Unfortunately (and fortunately) the surgery makes her cry out of her mouth. I believe this joke is a perfect joke. Funny in theory and thinking, and even funnier in Tina's execution. Plus it is hilariously visual. I'm jealous of whoever wrote this.

3. Chris Farley as Matt Foley

The best parts of the great book *Live from New York,* by Tom Shales, are when performers like Chris Rock, David Spade, and Adam Sandler talk about Chris Farley. They speak of their friend in the most reverential ways. Chris Rock says that when anyone ever asked him who was the funniest of the group there, it was always, always Chris Farley. I totally get it.

Matt Foley, the motivational speaker, is probably my favorite recurring *Saturday Night Live* character, ever. The level of commitment from Chris Farley is astounding, almost disturbing. The famous one, when he picks up David Spade like King Kong, and then later falls and smashes a coffee table, is one of the most deliriously funny things I've ever seen in my life.

4. Amy Poehler as Kaitlin

In just the past ten years or so, Amy Poehler has produced a lifetime's worth of awe-inspiring performances. Her hyperactive eleven-year-old Kaitlin is my favorite. There's an innocence to the performance that is such a surprise. Kaitlin's adventures with her subdued, kind, put-upon stepdad, Rick—played with the perfect amount of listlessness by Horatio Sanz—make me laugh but also make me want to take care of Kaitlin. One of my greatest pet peeves is women who infantilize themselves in real life, but I have a special place in my heart for women who can play little girls convincingly. Amy, all woman, all awesome, kicks ass as a little girl.

5. The Racial Draft on *Chappelle's Show*

If you watch this sketch, you can't believe it actually aired on television. The sketch portrayed all the races as professional teams, picking celebrities from a draft pool of all races to form the strongest race. *Chappelle's Show* did consistently edgy sketches that pushed the envelope with political and racial comedy but was so funny that it never got in trouble. So much can be excused if you're just funny enough. Sarah Silverman also has this rare gift. If I even inch toward making a race joke, it's so artlessly done someone immediately wants me removed from set.

6. Paul Rudd in *Wet Hot American Summer*

Paul Rudd plays the funniest dick boyfriend of all time in this movie. The scene in which he refuses to pick up a tray is the moment when Paul Rudd transformed in my eyes from handsome straight guy in a comedy movie to weirdo generator of awesome comedy in a handsome guy's body. His past performances as nice guy in *Clueless* and *Romeo + Juliet* make this turn especially unexpected and fun.

7. Ricky Gervais as David Brent

Only people who have seen the British *Office* will remember the moment when David Brent says, "I think there's been a rape up there" in a sensitivity training seminar he is holding. As my friend B. J. Novak described it, it was such a profoundly funny moment on television that there was a paradigm shift in comedy after he said it. With the character of David Brent, Ricky Gervais guaranteed that he would live in the pantheon forever, even if he did years of terrible, mediocre stuff. (I'm not saying he will, but he could if he wanted.) He's like Woody Allen, and the original *The Office* is his *Annie Hall*.

8. Christopher Moltisanti's Drug Intervention on *The Sopranos*

The Sopranos was one of the funniest shows ever, with a level of observational comedy that most comedies would kill for. This is the only drug intervention I have ever seen that ends in the person being "helped" getting beaten up by his loved ones.

9a. Frank the Tank Getting Shot in the Neck with a Tranquilizer in *Old School*

Sorry, so much Will Ferrell. I just love this guy so much. This series of moments is a masterpiece of editing and excellent blocking choices by Todd Phillips. Here's the sequence: Frank the Tank gets hit in the neck with an animal tranquilizer meant for a petting zoo animal. Groggy and heavily drugged, he meanders around a yard, knocking over a child's elaborate birthday cake. He then immediately falls into the pool—and while he's underwater, the movie is scored to the somber and dulcet Simon and Garfunkel's "Sounds of Silence," in homage to *The Graduate*. It's just a dense brownie of sweet comedy.

9b. Tied with Will Ferrell stabbing his own thigh with a knife to prove he's paralyzed in *Talladega Nights*

Just amazing.

10. Melissa McCarthy in *Bridesmaids*

Sometimes you watch something so funny you realize after the moment is over that you've stopped breathing. You're actually breathless. That's how I felt the first time I saw Melissa McCarthy in *Bridesmaids,* in the scene where she first meets Kristen Wiig's character and tells her she hasn't been doing so well because she "fell off a cruise ship," and then "hit every rail down," and finally "has several metal pins in her leg" from the experience. You don't often hear the words *captivating* and *gross* used to describe the same character in a movie, but Melissa McCarthy managed to evoke both in the very best ways. I could not keep my eyes off of her.

11. Michael Scott Hitting Meredith with His Car on *The Office*
In the history of the *The Office,* I believe the single funniest moment is when Michael Scott hits Meredith Palmer with his car, just as he's talking about how much he loves his employees. Our show may have a great writing staff and has written some fantastic jokes, and I have seen some amazingly funny acting on the show, but when Michael screams as Meredith's lifeless body hits his windshield, I just don't think anything else we've done is as purely funny as that. I think tribesmen in a remote jungle in the Congo would find this moment funny.

Some others:
Borat on the treadmill in *Da Ali G Show:* a star is born.

Michael Palin's massive stutter attack in *A Fish Called Wanda:* a tour de force. Everyone doing exactly what they do best at the same time.

Dwight Schrute capturing a bat in a trash bag around Meredith's head on *The Office:* a moment of tiny, hilarious violence.

Kristen Wiig's Bjork impression on *Saturday Night Live:* so recognizable and instantly funny while being completely over the top. Makes me wish Bjork were in the news more, just so I could see more of this impression.

How I Write

I LIVE IN a Spanish-style house in an area of Los Angeles near The Grove. The Grove is an outdoor shopping extravaganza with a fountain that shoots jets of water synchronized to Kool & the Gang songs. People love to hate on The Grove, but it's insanely popular. It's the mall equivalent of the Kardashian family. So, that's my neighborhood, and I have a cute little house in it. I really love it.

I bought my house during the famous writers' strike of 2007. You of course remember the strike because it was over the hot-button and nationally polarizing issue of percentage of Internet residuals accrued from online media in perpetuity. Doesn't thinking about it now just make your blood boil?! Obviously, no one outside of a small group of professional writers really gets what was going on there, but the point is I had a lot of time to do nothing but not work and hemorrhage my savings. When I wasn't Norma Rae-ing it up on the picket line, I spent the rest of my time decorating my house to look like something out of *Architectural Digest*—a kind of Santa Barbara meets artsy old lady vibe. I think I did only an adequate job, but I did manage to avoid some typical L.A.-house pitfalls: I'm proud to say I don't have a single vintage poster of some old-timey French product, or a statue of Buddha.

But what I'm most proud of is my beautiful office:

I built it and decorated it, and then I promptly never used it. It's important to me to have a museum-quality office, so when people or potential biographers come over they think that's where I write.

No, where I really write is here:

As you can see, when I write, I like to look like I'm recovering from tuberculosis. I sit in bed, my laptop resting on a blanket or a Notre Dame sweatshirt on my lap. I got the sweatshirt when I was there doing stand-up in 2006. (Where I bombed, by the way. Those kids hated me and my long, matronly rants against low-rise jeans. I did a three-college comedy tour with my *Office* costar Craig Robinson, who is hilarious, and a pro at performing at colleges. He plays the piano in his act, incorporating medleys of hit pop songs and then does a rendition of an original song he wrote called "Take Your Panties Off." I don't need to tell you that it's very funny and all the college kids wished he'd partnered up with a different *Office* cast member.)

The blanket/sweatshirt keeps the laptop from getting too hot and radiating my ovaries, which everyone knows makes your children come out with ADD. I almost always write alone in my house. I never have music on, because I can't concentrate with Nelly Furtado remixes thumping, and, unfortunately, I have only dance music on my iPod, which is how I got to be such a great dancer.

The main reason I enjoy working on a writing staff is because of the social nature of the job. To put it kindly, I am a very talkative, social person. To put it less kindly, I'm a flibbertigibbet, which is what my frenemy Rainn Wilson calls me. It's always been incredibly challenging for me to put pen to page, because writing, at its heart, is a solitary pursuit, designed to make people depressoids, drug addicts, misanthropes, and antisocial weirdos (see every successful writer ever except Judy Blume). I also have a nice office at work, but I use it primarily as a messy closet.

The Internet also makes it extraordinarily difficult for me to focus. One small break to look up exactly how almond milk is made, and four hours later I'm reading about the Donner Party and texting all my friends: DID YOU GUYS KNOW ABOUT THE DONNER PARTY AND HOW MESSED UP THAT WAS? TEXT ME BACK SO WE CAN TALK ABOUT IT!

My high school newspaper interviewed me a few years ago
and wanted a photo of me writing, so I had my coworker Dan Goor
take this of me looking polished and writerly at my work desk.
It is so fraudulent it makes me laugh.

I've found my productive-writing-to-screwing-around ratio to be one to seven. So, for every eight-hour day of writing, there is only one good productive hour of work being done. The other seven hours are preparing for writing: pacing around the house, collapsing cardboard boxes for recycling, reading the DVD extras pamphlet from the BBC *Pride & Prejudice,* getting snacks lined up for writing, and YouTubing toddlers who learned the "Single Ladies" dance. I know. Isn't that horrible? So, basically, writing this piece took me the time between Thanksgiving and Christmas. Enjoy it accordingly.

The Day I Stopped Eating Cupcakes

VERY RECENTLY I was out on script for *The Office* for a week. "Out on script" refers to when writers are sent off on their own to write a first draft of an episode of the show.

It is an amazing time, basically paid and sanctioned hooky. This means that instead of showering, dressing, and coming into work every day, I'm allowed to laze around my house in a giant T-shirt and no pants, or go shopping, or attend trendy cardio classes with my fun unemployed friends. Obviously this is the best time ever.*

This time when I was on script, I stopped by my favorite cupcake place, which I will call Sunshine Cupcakes. (Sunshine Cupcakes, while a ridiculous name, is actually a restrained parody of cupcake bakery names. You have no idea. In Los Angeles, cupcake bakeries are as pervasive as Starbucks. They are the product of a city with an abundance of trophy wives, because trophy wives are the financial engines of cutesy com-

---

* The other best time ever is lying on my back eating licorice, watching hours of a serialized sex-crime drama—oh, don't get all offended. It's an actual genre now; I didn't invent it—with my head resting on the sternum of an unwilling loved one.

merce that makes Los Angeles like no other American city: toe jewelry, doorknob cozies, vegan dog food, you get it. If I am sounding mean, I should tell you how envious and admiring I am of these trophy wives. I'd marry a partner at William Morris Endeavor and start a cat pedicure parlor m'self if I were so lucky.)

So, yeah, on my fourth consecutive visit to Sunshine Cupcakes, I was paying for my cupcake when the female manager (cupcake apron, Far Side glasses, streak of pink hair: the universal whimsical bakery lady uniform, as far as I can tell) approached me.

FAR SIDE: You've come here a lot this week.

ME (mouthful of a generous sample): Yeah, I love this place, man.

FAR SIDE: We know you're on Twitter. (Leaning in conspiratorially) And if you're willing to tweet about loving Sunshine Cupcakes, this cupcake (gesturing to the one I was buying) is free.

I did not know it was possible to be *triple* offended. First of all, Manager Woman, if you notice that a thirty-two-year-old woman is coming to your cupcake bakery every day for a week, keep that information to yourself. I don't need to be reminded of how poor my food choices are on a regular basis. Second, how cheap and/or poor do you think I am? A cupcake costs two bucks! You think I'm miserly enough to think, like, Oh goody, I can save those two bucks for some other tiny purchase later today! And third, even if I were to buy into this weird bribey situation where I endorse your product, you think the cost of it would be one measly cupcake? The implications of this offer were far worse than anything she meant to propose, obviously, but I hate her forever nonetheless.

This is why I never eat cupcakes anymore. The connotations are too disturbing. Lucky for me, the mighty doughnut is making a comeback. No one better ruin doughnuts for me, or I will be so pissed.

Somewhere in Hollywood
Someone Is Pitching This Movie

A FEW YEARS ago I sat down for a meeting with some executives at a movie studio that I will call Thinkscope Visioncloud. Thinkscope Visioncloud had put out some of my favorite movies and they wanted to hear some of my ideas, so I was naturally very excited. All television writers do is dream of one day writing movies. We long for the glitziness of the movie world. I'll put it this way: at the Oscars, the most famous person in the room is like, Angelina Jolie. At the Emmys, the big exciting celebrity is Kelsey Grammer, or *maybe* Helen Hunt if she decided to play Emily Dickinson or something in an HBO miniseries. Look, Frasier Crane is awesome, but you get what I'm trying to say. It's snobby and grossly aspirational, but it's true. So, I left work at *The Office* early one afternoon with a "See ya, suckers!" attitude and headed to my destiny.

The junior executive's office at Thinkscope Visioncloud was nicer than any room in a fifty-mile radius of *The Office* studio. The stuffed chair I was sitting on was expensive leather and looked like the one a judge would sit on in his private chamber on a TV show. I was so nervous the sweat from the back of my legs was making me stick to it. Oh yeah, I was wearing shorts to this meeting. What? For a television writer, this was a classy business casual outfit. After I finished sharing one of my ideas for a low-budget romantic comedy, I was met with silence. One of the execs sheepishly looked at the other execs.

EXEC: Yeah, we're really trying to focus in on movies about board games. People really seem to respond to those.

For the rest of the meeting we talked in earnest about if there was any potential in a movie called *Yahtzee!* I made some polite suggestions and left.

I am always surprised by what movie studios think people will want to see. I'm even more surprised how correct they are a lot of the time. The following movies are my best guess as to what may soon be coming to a theater near you:

- *Bananagrams 3D*
- *Apples to Apples 4D* (audiences are pummeled with apples at the end of the movie)
- *Crest Whitestrips*
- *Sharks vs. Volcanoes*
- *King Tut vs. King Kong*
- *Streptococcus vs. Candidiasis* (Strep Throat vs. Yeast Infection)
- *The Do-Over*
- *The Switcheroo*
- *Street Smart*
- *Street Stupid* (*Street Smart* sequel)
- *Fat Astronaut*
- *The Untitled Liam Neeson "You Took My Female Relative Project"*
- *The Untitled Jennifer Lopez Sonia Sotomayor Project*
- *Darling* (*Peter Pan* from the point of view of the Darling family's alcoholic dad)
- *The Bear from Those Toilet Paper Ads Movie 3D*
- *Gross Catastrophe*

- *Hate Fuck*
- *Fat Slut*
- *Sex Dude*
- *Bad Dog Walker* (You can see the poster already, can't you? Heather Graham in booty shorts, pulled in eight different directions by dogs on leashes and smiling a naughty grin.)
- *Grandpa Swap*
- *Stepmom Finishing School*
- *Human Quilt* (horror movie)
- *I Ain't Yo' Wife!*
- *You Ain't My Dad!*

As much as it may seem like I am mocking these movies, if any movie studio exec is reading this and is interested in any of the above, I will gladly take a meeting about them. I have an almost completed outline for *Crest Whitestrips*.

The Best Distraction
in the World:
Romance and Guys

Someone Explain One-Night Stands
to Me

I HAVE NEVER had a one-night stand. According to every women's magazine and television program ever made, this is super-unforgivably lame, and it behooves me to go reclaim my groove on an all-girls party trip to an unincorporated island territory of the United States. Every romantic comedy I watch depicts our adorable heroine walking sheepishly back from a stranger's place in the morning, with bedhead and her eyeliner all sexy and smudged. She might not yet have found Mr. Right (this is only the beginning of the movie), but she's having fun looking!

I just don't understand any of that at all. Here's why:

In my mind, the sexiest thing in the world is the feeling that you're wanted. The slightly nervous asking of your phone number. The text message asking you to dinner. The simple overture of wanting me can satisfy my ego for a good long time. The sexual situation that could come of it? Well, that's just less appealing to me. I don't mean to say I don't enjoy sex; I'm a properly functioning mammal and everything. I just think, like, who is this guy? Don't you need to know some more about a guy than an evening's worth of conversation at a bar to make sex appealing?

Also: fear is a pretty big turn-off. I'm talking about safety here. I don't even mean sexual health safety, like STDs. I mean good old-fashioned life-and-death safety. Here's what I can't wrap my brain around. I barely talk to strangers (a habit that I started as a child and that has served me well through my adulthood). So the idea of going to a stranger's house at night, or having that stranger over to my house, sounds insanely dangerous. These fears have made it so that when my female friends talk to me about one-night stands, I'm an incredibly irritating listener.

EXCITED SEXUALLY LIBERATED FRIEND: So, then it was like 2 a.m. that same night, and he knocked on my apartment door. I was in my robe and nothing else—

ME: No underwear?

EXCITED SEXUALLY LIBERATED FRIEND: No. I said "nothing else."

ME (skeptical): I feel like you were wearing underwear. That's how you are in, like, repose?

EXCITED SEXUALLY LIBERATED FRIEND: Yes.

ME: You really like not wearing underwear? Am I the only one who finds that totally uncomfortable? (lowered voice) Don't you ever sometimes . . . excrete?

EXCITED SEXUALLY LIBERATED FRIEND: Gross. Stop it.

ME: Okay. But let's remember to come back to this no-underwear conversation later.

EXCITED SEXUALLY LIBERATED FRIEND: So he knocked at the door—

ME: Wait! Sorry. I'm just realizing, your doorman let him up without ever seeing him before? Doesn't that disturb you, that your doorman would just let any old person off the street up to your apartment? I would give my doorman a book of photos of accepted guests that he could reference, like a reference book—

EXCITED SEXUALLY LIBERATED FRIEND: I'm doing fine with my doorman.

ME: I would have established a different procedure.

EXCITED SEXUALLY LIBERATED FRIEND: Great, Mindy. Anyway, then I showed him around the place—

ME: The doorman? (off ESL Friend's annoyed look) The guy! The guy! Yes.

EXCITED SEXUALLY LIBERATED FRIEND: He was into the way I decorated it. Really taking it in.

ME: He was casing the joint!

EXCITED SEXUALLY LIBERATED FRIEND: No! He was not casing the joint! He was being sexy and sweet and making cute little jokes about family photos. And then he asked if he could see my bedroom—

ME: Your bedroom, so he could rape and murder you!

Eventually, my constant interruptions make her so irritated, she stops telling her sexy story. I guess nothing puts a damper on a one-night stand as much as your friend pointing out all the opportunities where you might have been killed.

Don't get me wrong, I love hearing about it. I don't want to come off as prim or that I won't go see a R-rated movie or something. In fact, I would feel sad if I didn't have my Sexually Liberated Friend there to tell me fun, frank tales of desires fulfilled.

I just don't think I could ever do it myself.

So, this is what I'm like: if you come over to my house, I need to know your first and last name. I need to have your phone number and a person whom we both know so you can't disappear forever in case you murder me. Ultimately, it comes down to this: How embarrassing would it be for me to be talking to a detective at a precinct after you tried to rape and murder me in my home, and not be able to tell him your name or any information about you because we were having a one-night stand? I've seen *Law & Order: SVU*. I know how it works.

"Hooking Up" Is Confusing

THE CAREFUL reader will note that my teens and early twenties were largely without significant sexual incident. Okay, even the not-so-careful reader will notice this. All right. If you've merely glanced at the back cover of this book while you're in line at the bookstore, you'd probably come to that conclusion. This is what happens when you have friends who are more likely to tell ghost stories in a living room with flashlights than recount tales of raunchy sex encounters.

Because of this, I have fallen way behind in my terminology. I am especially tired of not knowing exactly what "hooking up" means. Some version of this happens to me constantly:

PSYCHED PAL: Oh, hey! I hooked up with Nikki last night.

ME: That's awesome! You've liked her for a while. Nice job.

(We high-five. A pause.)

ME: What does that mean? Did you have sex?

PSYCHED PAL: You're disgusting.

It's not that I'm some pervert looking for lurid details (this time, anyway). It's just that I have no idea what you are talking about. There have been times when friends have said they hooked up with someone and all it means is that they had a highly anticipated kissing session. Other times it's a full-on all-night sex-a-thon.* Can't we have a universal understanding of the term, once and for all? From now on, let's all agree that hooking up = sex. Everything else is "made out." And if you're older than twenty-eight, then just kissing someone doesn't count for crap and is not even worth mentioning. Unless you're Mormon, in which case you're going to hell. There, I think we're all on the same page. If Europe could figure out a way to do the euro, I feel confident we can do this.

---

* *Full-On All-Night Sex-a-Thon* is also the name of my debut hip-hop album.

I Love Irish Exits

I RECENTLY LEARNED that an "Irish exit" is when you leave a party without telling anyone (and presumably it is because you are too drunk to form words). A "French exit" is when you leave a party early without saying good-bye to anyone or paying your share of the bill and maybe you are also drunk. Um, I may have found these on kind of a xenophobic website. Makes me wonder about Jewish exits or Black exits. Okay, thin ice. Too far.

I think Irish exits should actually be de rigueur, except the drunk part. Slipping away is basically all I do now at large parties. My version of an Irish exit has an air of deception to it, because it includes my asking loudly, "Where's the bathroom?" and making theatrical looking-around gestures like a lost foreign tourist. But then, instead of finding the bathroom, I sneakily grab my coat and leave. Other times I say, "Oh, I think I left my lights on in my car!" or "Oh my gosh, I think I left my car unlocked." Cars make great pretexts for Irish exits. People never doubt weird issues you have with your car, because it's extremely boring to listen to.

The reason I pull Irish exits is not because I think I'm too busy and cool to be bothered with pleasantries. It's that when there is a gathering of more than thirty people I don't want to waste your time with hellos and good-byes. I think it's actually the more polite thing to do, because I'm not coercing partygoers into some big farewell moment with me. Then other people feel like they have to stop what they're doing and hug me, too. It's time-wasting dominoes.

Irish exits are supposed to be subtle, a way to leave without creating a disruption, and yes, on occasion, a way to perhaps escape notice for epic drunkenness. The only snag is you have to be comfortable lying directly to the faces of people you like. There has really been only one time when someone actually busted me on it. It occurred at my friend Louisa's birthday, on the roof of the Downtown Standard Hotel in L.A. when I was twenty-seven. I was having a crummy time because I was supposed to go with my friend Diana but she couldn't make it at the last minute because she was going to Burning Man.* Diana was going to be my wingwoman because I knew my ex-boyfriend was coming to the party with his new girlfriend, Chloe.

A word about Chloe: Chloe was so young (or young-looking) she'd actually played the daughter of an actress four years older than me on a TV show. But the worst thing about Chloe is that she was sweet.

Chloe approached me.

CHLOE (shyly): Can I just say you're my hero? I took the Long Island Rail Road out to see *Matt & Ben* when I was in middle school.

---

* I feel like I'm constantly being ditched for the Burning Man Festival. The Burning Man Festival is an annual festival that is an "experiment in human expression." Only something reprehensible would be so vague. There are only a few things that I've never actually done that I can say I categorically hate. One is Burning Man. The others are sky-diving, ménage à trois, and when parents tell stories about their babies and incorporate impressions of their babies' voices. I love hearing about your kid! Just use your normal voice!

Don't you dare, Chloe. Don't you dare make it impossible to hate you. Quit looking at me, all earnest, with those Bambi eyes. Also, I'm your "hero"? What am I, ten thousand years old? I quickly said something weird like "Bless you, child," excused myself, and walked briskly away. I went over to Louisa, who was standing with my friend Pete when I began to initiate an Irish exit.

ME: Oh man, you know what? I think I left my glove compartment open when I parked here. I'd better go check on it.

PETE: Just say you're leaving. We know you're not coming back.

Pete read my mind. At that moment, I was actually thinking about which twenty-four-hour taco stand on the drive back home would conceivably accept credit cards.

A word about Pete: Pete is a very funny, direct, mildly pessimistic guy who's a great friend because it's like Larry David is your pal. He's also one of those guys whose plainspokenness is charming when used on other people, but super irritating when used on you.

ME: I'm not leaving. Just need to check my car and maybe use the bathroom. Just drinking so much water these days. Health. Ha ha.

I mimed drinking a long gulp of water to sell the point.

PETE: Why must you always tell us why you're going to the bathroom?

Pete had a point. No one has ever been curious about what people do when they go to the bathroom. It was a sure sign of guilt: giving too much information about my cover story was such an amateur move.

Ugh! That stupid Chloe threw me off, with her hot young-ness and surprising sweetness. Why not just be a total bitch to me like I would've been if I had been the hot and young one? Damn it, Chloe!

Then I got an idea.

> ME: So am I trying to sneak out or am I using the bath-room, Pete? Get your idea of my motivations straight before you accuse me of something.

I looked around to see if anyone else had noticed my *Rainmaker*-level-closing-arguments rebuttal. Nope.

> PETE (not budging): You're obviously leaving.

> ME: Well, would someone who is sneaking out leave their coat here?

I slowly took off my jacket and, with a flourish, hurled it on a sofa. I looked at Pete triumphantly as I marched out of the room. I was still marching triumphantly as I walked down the hall, past the women's bathroom, into the elevator, across the lobby of the Standard to the street, where I got into my car and drove off.

The jacket was from Forever 21. Sorry, Pete, you don't know the freedom of the seventeen-dollar coat when caught at a party with an ex-boyfriend and his new hot girlfriend. And that, my friends, is how to execute an Irish exit. Thank you, Forever 21!

Guys Need to Do Almost Nothing
to Be Great

FORGIVE ME, but being a guy is so easy. A little Kiehl's, a
little Bumble and Bumble, a peacoat, and Chuck Taylors,
and you're hot.

Here's my incredibly presumptuous guide to being an awesome guy, inside and out. Mostly out, for who am I to instruct
you on inner improvement? Let me say here that if you're some
kind of iconoclastic dude who goes by the beat of your own
drum, you will find this insufferable. I totally understand this.
But why are you even reading this book at all? Shouldn't you be
hiking the Appalachian Trail right now or something?

1. Buy a well-fitting peacoat from J.Crew.
Or wait until Christmas sales are raging and buy a designer one,
like John Varvatos or something. Black looks good on everyone
(Obvious Cops) and matches everything (Duh Police), but charcoal gray is good, too. You can always look like a put-together
Obama speechwriter with a classy peacoat. Oh, and get it cleaned
once a year. Sounds prissy, but a good cleaning can return a peacoat to its true-black luster, and make you look as snappy as you
did on the first day you wore it.

2. Have a signature drink like James Bond.

It's silly, but I'm always so impressed if a guy has a cool go-to drink. Obviously, if it has a ton of fancy ingredients, like puréed berries or whatever, you can look a little bit like a high-maintenance weirdo, so don't do that. If you like Scotch, have a favorite brand. It makes you look all self-actualized and grown-up. (You don't have to say your drink order with the theatrical panache of James Bond. That's for close-ups.)

3. Own several pairs of dark-wash straight-leg jeans.

Don't get bootcut, don't get skinny—just a nice pair of Levi's, without any embellishments on the pockets. No embellishments anywhere. At all. Nothing. Oh my God.

4. Wait until all the women have gotten on or off an elevator before you get on or off.

Look, I'm not some chivalry nut or anything, but this small act of politeness is very visual and memorable.

5. When you think a girl looks pretty, say it.

But don't reference the thing that might reveal you are aware of the backstage process: e.g., say, "You look gorgeous tonight," not "I like how you did your makeup tonight." Also, a compliment means less if you compliment the thing and not the way the girl is carrying it off. So say, "You look so sexy in those boots," rather than "Those boots are really cool." I didn't make the boots! I don't care if you like the boots' design! We are magic to you: you have no idea how we got to look as good as we do.

6. Avoid asking if someone needs help in a kitchen or at a party, just start helping.

Same goes with dishes. (Actually, if you don't want to help, you should ask them if they need help. No self-respecting host or hostess will say yes to that question.)

7. Have one great cologne that's not from the drugstore.
Just one. Wear very little of it, all the time. I cannot tell you how sexy it is to be enveloped in a hug by a man whose smell you remember. Then, anytime I smell that cologne, I think of you. Way to invade my psyche, guy! Shivers down spine central!

8. Your girlfriend's sibling or parents might be totally nuts, but always defend them.
Always. All a girl wants to do is to get along with her family, and if you are on the side of making it easy, you will be loved eternally. It might be easier to condemn them—especially if she's doing that already—but, remarkably, even if they are murderers, she will find the good in them, *especially* if you start trashing them. Be the guy who says: "Hey, let's go visit your brother in prison on prison visiting day." Most likely she'll never make you actually do it, and she will always remember you offered.

9. Kiehl's for your skin, Bumble and Bumble for your hair.
Maybe a comb. That is all you need. And when girls look in your medicine cabinet (which they will obviously do within the first five minutes of coming to your place), you'll look all classily self-restrained because you'll have only two beauty products. You're basically a cowboy.

10. I really think guys only need two pairs of shoes.
A nice pair of black shoes and a pair of Chuck Taylors. The key, of course, is that you need to replace your Chuck Taylors every single year. You cannot be lax about this. Those shoes start to

stink like hell. They cost forty dollars. You can afford a new pair every year. And if you can't, why can't you? You have much bigger problems. Stop reading this and go deal with them.

11. Bring wine or chocolate to everything.
People love when guys do that. Not just because of the gift, but because it is endearing to imagine you standing in line at Trader Joe's before the party.

12. Get a little jealous now and again, even if you're not strictly a jealous guy.
Too much, and it's frightening, but a possessive hand on her back at a party when your girlfriend looks super hot is awesome.

Non-Traumatic Things
That Have Made Me Cry

I FEEL LIKE WE know each other pretty well by now. You've read about African kids bullying me, Broadway plays rejecting me, and my boss throwing me out of my place of employment. When I've cried about these things, the pain was real. So I guess I should actually feel grateful for all the times I cried from something that did not scar me emotionally. Isn't that what makes us wiser, or more interesting, or something? Nietzsche did a whole thing about this. Anyway, in addition to crying at typical girl cry-bait, like *The Notebook,* I also have been moved to tears by some other stuff, which I've listed in no particular order:

THE PROMISE OF EVAN LIEBERMAN

Just before Christmastime, when I was twenty-six, I met a really cool guy. I'll call him Evan. He was in finance and had been the college roommate of my friend Jeff, who worked on a sitcom I loved. Evan was smart, financially stable, and he loved comedy, even though he wasn't in comedy. We had roughly the same job description, which was that we both worked long hours at jobs we loved. Most notably, Evan was cheerful. It sounds odd, but cheerful is very hard to find in Los Angeles. I think sometimes people think cheerful is a synonym for dumb, so no one is ever cheerful. At that time I remember thinking, *I just want to meet a guy who has not been, at one point in his life, diagnosed with clinical depression.* That was my only criterion. Oh, and that he wouldn't make me convert religions if things got serious. (One thing you should know about me: I absolutely refuse to stop being a culturally Hindu, deeply superstitious Christmas tree have-r.) Evan was very exciting. For our first date, he took me to a really cool Korean BBQ place in K-Town he had clearly researched and driven by beforehand. That kind of apparent effort slays me. Over dinner Evan told lots of slightly embarrassing and funny stories about himself. He loved *The Office* and had seen exactly half the episodes, which was the perfect amount to me, for some reason. He was funny in a natural way. Plus he was super cute, in a "handsomest guy in the AP calculus class" kind of way, if that makes sense.

Do guys have any real idea how much time girls spend getting ready for a promising date? For my second date with Evan, I spent the afternoon getting my eyebrows waxed and my nails done, and spent a fortune at Fred Segal on a new skirt and even more time making the salespeople all weigh in on it. I honestly don't understand how people go on dates on weeknights; don't they want all that fun time before to get ready? I had kept all my best friends updated about my upcoming date in a long and exhaustively detailed e-mail chain with the subject heading: "HOLY SHIT YOU GUYS, MAY NOT TURN INTO A CRAZY JANE EYRE ATTIC LADY AFTER ALL." I really enjoy all these rituals; it's part of the fun of having a good date to look forward to. But it takes a lot of time and effort.

At six-thirty that night, I was standing in my bathroom with my hair in curlers—it's true: pink curlers, like in a Doris Day movie—when Evan texted (texted!) to cancel dinner because he wasn't "feeling well." No details of his sickness, no apologetic eagerness to set a new date, nothing. Just a vague and short text that ended with a ☹. It was less than an hour before he was supposed to pick me up.

I started crying almost immediately. A remarkable thing about me is that the time that elapses between a sad thought and a flood of tears is three or four seconds. I felt so foolish, having spent so much time (and money!) getting ready. Besides the pain of the rejection, he was also robbing me of a fun evening, getting taken out, a good-night kiss, and of updating my "HOLY SHIT YOU GUYS, MAY NOT TURN INTO A CRAZY JANE EYRE ATTIC LADY AFTER ALL." correspondence with an exuberant reply-all. It sounds trite, and it is, but it is so hard to meet anyone I would even consider spending time alone with, so it was a painful blow that it was over as quickly as it had begun. I sent a new e-mail to my friends, by only changing the subject heading to "HE BAILED VIA TEXT. CONSIDERING MORPHINE ADDICTION TO EASE PAIN." My friends all called and texted within minutes with the appropriate "Fuck that guy!" messages.

As for Evan, I texted back a breezy "No worries! Feel better." text to save face. Evan thanked me for being cool about it, and I never heard from him again.

VALET GUYS WHO ARE MY DAD'S AGE

I can't even deal with this. When I see a man who is around my father's age running down the street to get a car, it breaks my heart.

THE ALBUM *GRACELAND*

In 2004, when I started working at *The Office* and had no friends, I would listen to *Graceland* and just weep. On the way to work, on the way home. And not just the more ballad-y songs about loss, like "Graceland." I even cried to "You Can Call Me Al."

The secret I learned is that albums that remind me of my childhood happiness make me incredibly sad now. I only have perfect memories of singing along to *Graceland* with my parents on long car rides to Virginia Beach to visit my parents' friends. It's sort of my go-to stock image of my childhood, actually. I think it has something to do with knowing I'll never be able to go back to that time that makes me cry every time I listen to it.

DEPRESSING ZEITGEISTY MAGAZINE ARTICLES ABOUT RELATIONSHIPS

Every couple months or so, some boundary-breaking article comes out in a nationally published magazine. The article makes a big thesis statement about relationships, like, say, how women don't need men anymore, or how if you're a woman over thirty-five you should just settle with whatever guy is halfway nice to you, or how monogamy is not feasible or plausible or enjoyable for any human and we should all be swingers, or a study is released that says you don't have to love your kids anymore or something. They're the kind of articles that are e-mailed everywhere, and I get them forwarded to me about eight times.

I'll read one of these articles, and immediately after I'm so swept up in it that I can't help but think, *Yes, yes, that is 100 percent right. Finally! Someone has confirmed that little voice in the back of my mind that has always not loved my kids! Or I'm so happy I'm this much closer to that swinging lifestyle I've been secretly craving! I'm normal! And now it's a national discussion, so others agree, and I can feel normal now.* But then, a week later, I'm thinking, *I hate this. I feel awful.* This wretched little magazine article has helped convince more open-minded liberal arts graduates that the nuclear family doesn't exist without some hideous twist, like the dad is allowed to go to an S&M dungeon once a week or something. It makes me cry because it means that fewer and fewer people are believing it's cool to want what I want, which is to be married and have kids and love each other in a monogamous, long-lasting relationship.

MARK DARCY

All women love Colin Firth: Mr. Darcy, Mark Darcy, George VI—at this point he could play the Craigslist Killer and people would be like, "Oh my God, the Craigslist Killer has the most boyish smile!" I love Colin Firth in everything, even as the obsessed, miffed, tortured non-Ralph Fiennes husband in *The English Patient*. But the role that makes me cry is Mark Darcy, from *Bridget Jones's Diary*.

When we first meet Mark, he's kind of a, well, dick. He's arrogant and judgmental and seems to take himself so seriously. But he is secretly wonderful (and not so secretly gorgeous). There is a part in the movie—I've seen it six or seven times, and I swear to God, every time I see it coming, I start tearing up in anticipation—when we first see that Mark Darcy is not a bad guy. In fact, we see that he is the best guy ever.

Do you guys remember the scene when Bridget is sneaking out of the horrible couples dinner, having humiliated herself in front of all of her "smug marrieds"? And when she's at the door, Mark stops her and he says, "I like you, very much. Just as you are."

It's ridiculous that I love this so much. It's so simple. It's not a witty, perfectly phrased, Ephron-y declaration by our charming, neurotic hero. It's so . . . plain. But the idea is the most beautiful thing in the world. So, obviously, it makes me cry.

A CHARLIE BROWN CHRISTMAS SOUNDTRACK ALBUM

If I ever get cast in some *Changeling*-type movie where I need to cry instantly because my child was murdered, I will make sure to have Vince Guaraldi's *A Charlie Brown Christmas* album ready to go in my trailer. The children's voices and connections to the Peanuts from my childhood are just the beginning. (I always identified with Peppermint Patty, in case you were wondering— the loud, opinionated man-girl who chased around her crush without even fully knowing she liked him.) The music is gorgeous, but even the upbeat arrangements are tinged with something sad, like Joni Mitchell's *Blue*.

JONI MITCHELL'S *BLUE*

I know every single word to this album, but you would never know that, because I blubber through the entire thing. Also, I find it extremely impossible not to cry when I hear Stevie Nicks's "Landslide," especially the lyric: "I've been afraid of changing, because I've built my life around you." I think a good test to see if a human is actually a robot/android/cylon is to have them listen to this song lyric and study their reaction. If they don't cry, you should stab them through the heart. You will find a fusebox.

IF MY MOM CRIES

It makes absolutely no difference what it is about, but if my mother is crying, I will start to cry. I think it mostly has to do with the fact that my mom never cries. She is so cool. Me, on the other hand, I cry like five times a week. My mom and I went to go see *The Help*, and during the movie I noticed her start tearing up. It was such a rare sight, I started to as well. Soon we were both weeping so hard it was as though we'd been black maids in Jim Crow–era Mississippi and the movie had hit too close to home. People were weirded out.

Jewish Guys

FIRST, A disclaimer: I know many racist people say: "But some of my best friends are black!" before they go off on a long, racist rant. This does not count as an excuse for racism anymore. I get it. However, I think I have a different circumstance. *All* of my best friends are Jewish. Doesn't that let me say whatever I want? I sure hope so, because I have a lot to say.

DON'T BE SUCH HYPOCHONDRIACS

What? I have a cold. Don't get a look of terror on your face. The worst that could happen is that you'll get a cold, too. You don't have to theatrically Purell a thousand times a day and look all panicky every time I come into the room.

Also, in the unlikely event that you do get sick, you do not have to give everyone a play-by-play, as though none of us has ever been sick before, or as though there were some suspense in the story of your cold, with twists and turns. ("I woke up this morning feeling pretty good, only to take a terrible turn for the worse after lunch!") I know this story. You get better. It works out.

BUT WHAT IF IT'S MORE THAN A COLD?

It's not. It's just a cold.

HIRING SOMEONE TO HANG UP A PICTURE
ON YOUR WALL

Is it as bad as hiring a guy to have sex with your wife? No, it's not as bad as that. But you get my point. I'm sorry I said that. Fine, hire a guy to hang up a picture on your wall. Fine, fine, fine. I don't know how to get it exactly straight, either.

THANKS FOR BEING SO INTO INDIAN FOOD

In college all the non-Jewish guys would treat Indian food as though it were an exotic anomaly to be greeted with "ooohs" and "aaahs." I like that when we go to an Indian restaurant you don't look over the menu pleadingly and ask if I will "just order for both of us?"

LARRY DAVID

I get mad about your perceived special connection with him. Like when you give that knowing chuckle and say, "Oh, Larry," like he's some incorrigible friend of your dad's from temple. We both know him from watching him on his show, which we watched together, at the same time.

ISRAEL

Israel is interesting, but every time we talk about it, it has to be for, like, two hours. I want to talk about it, but it can't be for two hours!

I HAVE A MOM TOO

Hey, look. I know you talk to your mom twice a day on the phone, and I talk to my mom only once a day. That doesn't mean your mom beats my mom. Also, I know your mom is an amazing cook. I feel like you think my mom cooked us Hamburger Helper growing up.

When you talk to me about your mom and how great she is, I listen respectfully and say, "Wow, she really does sound great." But when I talk about my mom, you kind of glaze over, like I'm some delusional kid talking about how I'm going to be president someday. You can't muster up even the slightest bit of acknowledgment that anybody else's mom could come close to being as funny, artsy, nurturing, and irreverent as your mom.

EXCEPT EZEKIEL, RAHM, AND ARI EMANUEL'S MOM

We both agree. She's incredible. She can do whatever she wants.

NATALIE PORTMAN

I know a small part of you thinks you could've ended up with Natalie Portman if you had played things a little differently. That's nice. You can have that. That's not hurting anybody.

Men and Boys

SOMETIMES I bring a script I'm working on to a restaurant and sit near people and eavesdrop on them. I could rationalize it—*Oh, this is good anthropological research for characters I'm writing*—but it's basically just nosiness. I especially like eavesdropping on women my age. Besides being titillating, it also helps me gauge where I'm at in comparison. Am I normal? Am I doing the correct trendy cardio exercises? Am I reading the right books? Is gluten still lame? Is soap cool again, or is body wash still the way to go? It was through eavesdropping that I learned that you could buy fresh peanut butter at Whole Foods from a machine that *grinds it in front of you.* I had wasted so much of my life eating stupid old, already-ground peanut butter. So, yeah, I highly recommend a little nosiness once in a while.

Once, at BLD, a restaurant where I was writing, I saw two attractive thirty-ish women talking over brunch. They had finished eating and were getting seconds on coffee, so I knew it was going to be good.

I heard the following:

GIRL #1 (pretty Jewish girl, Lululemon yoga pants, great
   body): Jeremy just finished his Creative Writing pro-

gram at Columbia. But now he wants to maybe apply to law school.

GIRL #2 (tiny Asian girl, sheet of black hair, strangely huge breasts [for an Asian girl]): Oh God.

LULULEMON: What?

32D: How many grad schools is he going to go to?

LULULEMON: I know. But it's not his fault. No publishers are buying short stories from unfamous people. Basically you have to be Paris Hilton to sell books these days.

32D: For the past ten years that Jeremy has been out of college doing entry-level job after entry-level job and grad school, you've had a job that has turned into a career.

LULULEMON: Yeah, so?

32D: Jeremy's a boy. You need a man.

Lululemon did not take this well, as I anticipated.

I felt bad for Lulu because I've been Lulu. It's really hard when you realize the guy you've been dating is basically a high schooler at heart. It makes you feel like Mary Kay Letourneau. It's the worst.

Until I was thirty, I only dated boys, as far as I can tell. I'll tell you why. Men scared the shit out of me.

Men know what they want. Men make concrete plans. Men own alarm clocks. Men sleep on a mattress that isn't on the floor. Men tip generously. Men buy new shampoo instead of adding water to a nearly empty bottle of shampoo. Men go to the dentist. Men make reservations. Men go in for a kiss without giving you some long preamble about how they're thinking of kissing you. Men wear clothes that have never been worn by anyone else before. (Okay, maybe men aren't exactly like this. This is what I've cobbled together from the handful of men I know or know of, ranging from Heathcliff Huxtable to Theodore Roosevelt to my dad.) Men know what they want and they don't let you in on their inner monologue, and that is scary.

Because what I was used to was boys.

Boys are adorable. Boys trail off their sentences in an appealing way. Boys bring a knapsack to work. Boys get haircuts from their roommate, who "totally knows how to cut hair." Boys can pack up their whole life in a duffel bag and move to Brooklyn for a gig if they need to. Boys have "gigs." Boys are broke. And when they do have money, they spend it on a trip to Colorado to see a music festival. Boys don't know how to adjust their conversation when they're talking to their friends or to your parents. They put parents on the same level as their peers and roll their eyes when your dad makes a terrible pun. Boys let your parents pay for dinner when you all go out. It's assumed.

Boys are wonderful in a lot of ways. They make amazing, memorable, homemade gifts. They're impulsive. Boys can talk for hours with you in a diner at three in the morning because they don't have regular work hours. But they suck to date when you turn thirty.

I'm thirty-two and I fully feel like an adult. Sure, sometimes I miss wearing Hello Kitty jewelry or ironic T-shirts from Urban Outfitters on occasion. Who doesn't? I don't, because I think it would seem kind of pitiful. But a guy at thirty-two—he can act and dress like a grown man or a thirteen-year-old boy, and both are totally acceptable. Not necessarily to me, but to most people. (I can't tell you how many thirty- and fortysomething guys wear Velcro shoes in Los Angeles. It's an epidemic.) That's one of the weirdest things I've noticed about being thirty-two. It is a lot of women and a lot of boys our age. That's why I started getting interested in men.

When I was twenty-five, I went on exactly four dates with a much older guy whom I'll call Peter Parker. I'm calling him Peter Parker because the actual guy's name was also alliterative, and because, well, it's my book and I'll name a guy I dated after Spider-Man's alter ego if I want to.

Peter Parker was a comedy writer who was a smidgen more accomplished than me but who talked about everything with the tone of "you've got a lot to learn, kid." He had been a writer at a pretty popular sitcom. He gave me lots of unsolicited advice about how to get a job "if *The Office* got canceled." After a while, it became clear that he thought *The Office* would get canceled, and on our fourth and last date, it was clear that he thought *The Office* should get canceled.

Why am I bringing up Peter Parker? Well, besides moonlighting as Spider-Man, Peter was the first man I dated. An insufferable, arrogant man, but a legit man.

Peter owned a house. It wasn't ritzy or anything, just a little Spanish ranch-style house in Hollywood. But he was the first guy I'd dated who'd really moved into his place and made it a home. The walls were painted; there was art in frames. He had installed a flat-screen TV and speakers. There was just so much screwed into the walls. Everywhere I looked I saw another instance of an action that, if the house were a rental, would make you lose your deposit. I marveled at the brazenness of it. Peter's house reminded me more of my house growing up than of a college dorm room. I'd never seen that before.*

Owning a house obviously wasn't enough to make me want to keep dating Peter. Like I said, he was kind of a condescending

---

* Look, I'm not an idiot, I realize plenty of boys own houses. That's, like, the whole point of the Playboy mansion.

dick. But I observed in Peter a quality that I found really appealing and that I knew I wanted in the next guy I dated seriously: a guy who wasn't afraid of commitment.

At this point you might want to smack me and say: "Are you seriously another grown woman talking about how she wants a man who isn't afraid of commitment? Is this a book, or a blog called *Ice Cream Castles in the Air: One Single Gal Hopes for Prince Charming*? We've all heard this before!" But let me explain! I'm not talking about commitment to romantic relationships. I'm talking about commitment to things: houses, jobs, neighborhoods. Having a job that requires a contract. Paying a mortgage. I think when men hear that women want a commitment, they think it means commitment to a romantic relationship, but that's not it. It's a commitment to not floating around anymore. I want a guy who is entrenched in his own life. Entrenched is awesome.

So I'm into men now, even though they can be frightening. I want a schedule-keeping, waking-up-early, wallet-carrying, non-Velcro-shoe-wearing man. I don't care if he has more traditionally "men problems" like having to take prescription drugs for cholesterol or hair loss. I can handle it. I'm a grown-up too.

In Defense of Chest Hair

A S A THIRTEEN-YEAR-OLD, my big celebrity crush was Pierce Brosnan. Yeah, I know. Pierce Brosnan is such an uncreative crush that it sounds like the panicked choice of a closeted lesbian teenager. But, Pierce was my guy. I was thirteen and watching *Mrs. Doubtfire* in the theater with all my friends. There is a scene in which Pierce Brosnan gets out of a pool, Cheryl Tiegs–style. He is manly and glistening, and I remember this one point very clearly: he has a thick swatch of chest hair. It was a minor sexual awakening. During *Mrs. Doubtfire.* Not a movie often cited for its idealized depiction of traditional masculinity.

I have always liked a man with chest hair. I have only fond memories of my dad's as a kid, peeking out of a really cool button-up shirt he wore with a map of the world on it. I think chest hair looks distinguished. It's, like, cool—my dad's a man.

So I really don't understand why men shave or wax their chests. I find it so unnecessary. I mean, I sort of get it if you're a professional swimmer because each hair follicle adds a second to your time or something, but it's every single male actor in Hollywood. When I turn on an hour-long drama and all I see are these forty-year-old men with hairless chests, I feel slightly nauseated. Why? For the same reason one might feel nauseated by a woman with too many cosmetic injectables in her face: it just shows so much icky effort to conform to some arbitrary beauty standard. And the standard in this instance is particularly insane. You want to strip your body of something that is so coolly and distinctly male? Yuck! When I see a perfectly hairless, tanned guy on-screen, I am forced to recall the Chihuahua. Or I think of the process by which the man got rid of his chest hair. How much did it cost to get waxed? Will it grow out into prickly stubble? And frankly, guys, you should be suspect of these gals who are like va-va-va-voom over your smooth, hair-free chest. She must want you to look like either a Chippendale (who are all gay anyway, as everyone knows) or a little boy.

Look, I know the male equivalent of the person with my opinion is that creepy guy who declares he loves women to be "au natural" with a gross glint in his eye. But I'd rather be a female version of that guy than not say this at all. Besides, I've already revealed myself to be a bit of a creep in several sections of this book. Please leave your chest hair alone!

Married People Need to Step It Up

PRETTY MUCH the only thing I remember from my Shake-speare course in college is that one can identify a comedy, as opposed to a tragedy, because it ends in a wedding. (I also remember that weird play *The Winter's Tale*, where a woman poses as a statue for years or something. I remember thinking, *What am I reading? This is* ridiculous. *Take this off the syllabus!*) That's also how, I've noticed, most romantic comedies end. But I think the actual reason Shakespeare ended them there is because he thought the journey leading up to marriage was more fun to watch than the one that begins after the vows were said.

Growing up, I would say about 25 percent of the kids I knew had divorced parents. It wasn't out of the ordinary at all, and in fact, it was kind of glamorous. You never knew which parent's house you were going to have a sleepover at, and you hoped it was the dad's. The dad's house always had cable TV or a pool, and he ordered out for dinner instead of cooking.

As an adult, I've met an ocean of divorced people. I might even know more divorced people than married people, because I live in godless Los Angeles, where if you're engaged it simply means you're publicly announcing that you are dating a person monogamishly.

I also became familiar with an entirely new category of people: the unhappily married person. They are everywhere, and they are ten thousand times more depressing than a divorced person. My friend Tim, whose name I've changed, obviously, has gotten more and more depressing since he married his girlfriend of seven years. Tim is the kind of guy who corners you at a party to tell you, vehemently, that *marriage is work*. And that you have to *work on it constantly*. And that going to couples' therapy is not only normal but something that everyone needs to do. Tim has a kind of manic, cult-y look in his eye from paying thousands of dollars to a marriage counselor. He is convinced that his daily work on his marriage, and his acknowledgment that it is basically a living hell, is modern. The result is that he has helped to relieve me of any romantic notions I had about marriage.

What is fascinating to me is that divorced people tend to be the least depressing or depressed people I know. They're all unburdened and cleansed, and the wiser for it. This is the case even if they didn't initiate the divorce. I have a comedy writer friend, Sandy, whose husband left her for another woman the moment his restaurant (which Sandy had invested in and made possible) became successful. It was kind of the worst story anyone had ever heard, a betrayal that, had it happened to me, I would've driven slowly around downtown Los Angeles at night in my car with my windows rolled down, trying to solicit a hit man to murder my husband. After six months of hardship and going to therapy three times a week, Sandy's now elated. She realized— as has almost everyone I know who has been left or broken up with—that, by divorcing her, her husband relieved her of the job of eventually leaving *him*. As my mom has said, when one person is unhappy, it usually means two people are unhappy but that one has not come to terms with it yet. Sandy hadn't realized how unhappy she was until he was gone. She told me that her husband's leaving her was the nicest gift he ever gave her, because she would never have seen clearly enough to do it herself. It's not easy, of course; they have kids, and coordinating and sharing them is a hassle and a heartbreak. But she's still better off than she was before.

A COUPLE OF GREAT MARRIAGES

My parents get along because they are pals. They're not big on analyzing their relationship. What do I mean by pals? It mostly means they want to talk about the same stuff all the time. In my parents' case, it's essentially rose bushes, mulch, and placement of shrubs. They love gardening. They can talk about aphids the way I talk about New York Fashion Week. They can spend an entire day together talking nonstop about rhododendrons and *Men of a Certain Age,* watch Piers Morgan, and then share a vanilla milkshake and go to bed. They're pals. (Note: they are pals, not best friends. My mom's best friend is her sister. A best friend is someone you can talk to ad nauseam about feelings, clothing, and gossip. My dad is completely uninterested in that.)

Not to belabor the Amy Poehler of it all, but I've always really admired her marriage to Will Arnett. I remember at the *Parks and Recreation* premiere four years ago, Amy was looking for her husband toward the end of the night. She stopped by me and a couple other *Office* writers who had scammed invites to the party.

AMY: Hey guys. Have you seen Arnett? I can't find him.

We didn't know where he was, and she shook her head good-naturedly, like, "That guy," and went on looking for him. I had never heard a woman call her husband by his last name, like she was a player on the same sports team Will was on. You could tell from that small moment that Will and Amy are total pals.

C'MON, MARRIED PEOPLE

I don't want to hear about the endless struggles to keep sex exciting, or the work it takes to plan a date night. I want to hear that you guys watch every episode of *The Bachelorette* together in secret shame, or that one got the other hooked on *Breaking Bad* and if either watches it without the other, they're dead meat. I want to see you guys high-five each other like teammates on a recreational softball team you both do for fun. I want to hear about it because I know it's possible, and because I want it for myself.

I guess I think happiness can come in a bunch of forms, and maybe a marriage with tons of work makes people feel happy. But part of me still thinks...is it really so hard to make it work? What happened to being pals? I'm not complaining about Romance Being Dead—I've just described a happy marriage as based on talking about plants and a canceled Ray Romano show and drinking milkshakes: not exactly rose petals and gazing into each other's eyes at the top of the Empire State Building or whatever. I'm pretty sure my parents have gazed into each other's eyes maybe once, and that was so my mom could put eyedrops in my dad's eyes. And I'm not saying that marriage should always be easy. But we seem to get so gloomily worked up about it these days. In the Shakespearean comedies, the wedding is the end, and there isn't much indication of what happily ever after will look like day to day. In real life, shouldn't a wedding be an awesome party you throw with your great pal, in the presence of a bunch of your other friends? A great day, for sure, but not the beginning and certainly not the end of your friendship with a person you can't wait to talk about gardening with for the next forty years.

Maybe the point is that any marriage is work, but you may as well pick work that you like. Writing this book is work, but it's fun work, and I picked it and I enjoy doing it with you, Reader. It's my job, and it's a job I like. Tim, on the other hand, had chosen a very tough and kind of bad-sounding job, like being the guy who scrapes barnacles off the pylons of an oil rig in the frigid Arctic Sea.

Married people, it's up to you. It's entirely on your shoulders to keep this sinking institution afloat. It's a stately old ship, and a lot of people, like me, want to get on board. Please be psyched, and convey that psychedness to us. And always remember: so many, many people are envious of what you have. You're the star at the end of the Shakespearean play, wearing the wreath of flowers in your hair. The rest of us are just the little side characters.

Why Do Men
Put on Their Shoes So Slowly?

I HAVE A serious question, and it is a sexist question. But it is a pretty gentle and specific form of sexist question, so I think it's okay.

Why do all the men I know put their shoes on incredibly slowly? When I tie my shoelaces I can do it standing, and I'm out the door in about ten seconds. (Or, more often, I don't even tie my shoelaces. I slip my feet into my sneakers and tighten the laces in the car.) But with men, if they are putting on *any* kind of shoe (sneaker, Vans, dress shoe), it will take twenty times as long as when a woman does it. It has come to the point where if I know I'm leaving a house with a man, I can factor in a bathroom visit or a phone call or both, and when I'm done, he'll almost be done tying his shoes.

There's a certain meticulousness that I notice with all guys when they put their shoes on. First of all, they sit down. I mean, they need to sit down to do it. Right there, it signals, "I'm going to be here for a while. Let's get settled in." I can put on a pair of hiking boots that have not even been laced yet while talking on my cell phone, without even leaning on a wall.

I don't have any real problems with it, except when you've done a whole snappy/sexy exit conversation with a guy leaving your place and then he tacks on an extra eight minutes as he puts on his shoes.

My Appearance:
The Fun and
the Really Not Fun

When You're Not Skinny, This Is What People Want You to Wear

GETTING PROFESSIONALLY beautified was all that I dreamed about doing when I was an asexual-looking little kid. That's because my parents dressed both my brother and me according to roughly exactly the same aesthetic: Bert from Ernie and Bert. Easing them out of dressing me in primary colors and cardigans (seriously, I was a child who wore *cardigans*) and getting them to let me grow my hair out past my earlobes was a first huge step that took years.

Cosby sweater on, lovin' life.

So, yeah, now that I'm an adult, getting made beautiful by a team of professionals for a red carpet event or a magazine photo shoot is heaven to me. The part that is not fun is someone picking out clothes for me.

I love shopping and fashion, as anyone who has read more than a paragraph of this book will know. But for magazine photo shoots and things, they hire stylists for me, because they have a certain idea for how they want me to look, and it isn't necessarily how I would style myself, which is 1980s-era Lisa Bonet.

Since I am not model skinny, but also not super fat and fabulously owning my hugeness, I fall in that nebulous "normal American woman" size that legions of fashion stylists detest. For the record, I'm a size eight (this week, anyway). Many stylists hate that size, because I think, to them, it shows that I lack the discipline to be an ascetic or the confident sassy abandon to be a total fatty hedonist. They're like: pick a lane! Just be so enormous that you need to be buried in a piano, and dress accordingly.

For the record, they're not all bad. I've worked with some really badass stylists who make me look so smokin' hot your face would melt. Monica Rose, who styled me for this book cover, totally gets my body and celebrates it. (Yes, I say things like "celebrates my body" like your old hippie aunt.) But many stylists don't know what to do with me.

Over the past seven years, here's what stylists have tried to make me wear:

Navy: Ah, navy, the thin-lipped, spinster sister of black. Black, though chic and universally slimming, is considered a boring red carpet color and is rarely featured on best-dressed lists. That's why I get shown a lot of navy. Navy has made a comeback in the past few years, which is terrific, because before that, navy was most famous as the signature color for postal workers.

Cap sleeves: Cap sleeves look good on no one, and yet I am given them all the time. I believe it is in an effort to hide the flesh where my arm meets my torso, which I guess is disgusting. Cap sleeves should be worn exclusively by toddler flower girls at a wedding.

Billowing bohemian blouses billed as "Poet tops": Skinny girls like Mary Kate and Ashley Olsen look ethereal and gorgeous in hippie clothes with lots of volume. I love the bohemian look, but when I try it, I look like a chubby gypsy. Also, chubby people can never truly pull off ethereal the same way skinny people can never be jolly. The only fat ethereal person I can think of was Anna Nicole Smith, and in her case, ethereal might have meant "drugged."

Layers of chunky beaded necklaces: Nothing makes me look like a social worker from the 1970s like several layers of colorful, conspicuous, statement necklaces.

Muumuus: In college, I was cast in a student-written musical that was a retelling of a Greek myth. It was a very cool play with a small cast, each of whom played several roles. The costume designer, an always-frowning girl named Stephanie, had us in for a fitting. She gave tight black unitards to every other actor, so when they played different roles, they could layer simple costume pieces over them and become the new character. I loved the idea. Then it was my turn to get fitted. I was given an enormous, shapeless black muumuu held together by a wad of Velcro and tied together with gold rope. It was obvious it had been made out of the same material as the black canvas curtains of the stage. Stephanie (not a skinny girl herself, by the way) so clearly didn't want to "deal" with my body. When I complained to the director, he talked to her. She was furious, saying I was "a difficult fit." I did not know Stephanie would be the first of many people who would throw a muumuu on me and call it a day.

Shawls: I routinely get shawls draped on me, as though I am Queen Elizabeth. A routine injustice done to the non-thin is to make them look like creaky old ladies.

Sherlock Holmes–style cloaks: This I don't mind so much, as long as I have a pipe and a monocle.

Ponchos: Nothing says "English is not my first language" like me in a poncho.

Billowing pants: Once, a stylist for a famous women's fashion magazine dressed me in massive charcoal gray pants with a drawstring. They looked like something a sad clown might wear running errands. Maternity tops billed as "Grecian style" are a relative of billowing pants.

Daisy print: I think there's something about daisies or daisy prints that stylists consider synonymous with "cheerful, simple, fat woman."

Honestly, I feel like some stylists would put me in a hot dog costume and try to convince me that in Paris all the girls are dressing like the Oscar Mayer wiener, just to cover up my body.

In 2011, *People* magazine named me one of the Most Beautiful English-Speaking Persons in North America, in a countrywide vote where I just fucking destroyed. But I don't need to remind you of this; you probably have the page torn out and stuck on your fridge as inspiration. In all seriousness, it was an amazing surprise, and I was very flattered and excited. I would even say it was an honor to be singled out for my looks, but I don't think

I could in good conscience write something that silly in a book that teenage girls might read.

In case you thought the photo shoot that produced that image in *People* went seamlessly—pun intended and relished—here's what happened:

The photo shoot took place on a Saturday at a public elementary school about an hour away from Hollywood. As I drove there, I got more and more excited, chatting with my mom and promising her I'd send photos. I was set to do the shoot with my *Office* costar Ellie Kemper, who is a close friend and one of my favorite people.

A charismatic and almost incomprehensible French stylist took me to a trailer filled with gowns. It was like walking through Saddam Hussein's niece's closet. Organza, tulle, and silk filled the trailer from floor to ceiling; rhinestones and feathers were everywhere. Each gown was more elaborate and gorgeous than the one before. And they were all a size zero.

The stylist had not brought any non-samples. The only thing that came close to my size was a shapeless navy shift, which I didn't want to wear because of my aforementioned feelings about navy, and also because it looked like what Judi Dench might wear to the funeral of someone she didn't care that much about. I looked around for other options. There were none.

I excused myself by saying I needed to use the bathroom, which, since we were shooting in an elementary school, was the same one the kids used during the day. I went into a stall, sat down on a kid-size toilet, and cried. Why didn't I just lose twenty pounds so I never had to be in this situation again? Life was so much easier for the actresses who did that. Was my problem that I was this food monster destined to only wear navy shifts? Lots of stupid people were skinny, and yet I couldn't do this incredibly simple thing they could do with seeming ease.

I reached for some toilet paper to wipe my tears and saw that the dispenser was empty. I sighed and went to the next stall. No toilet paper. I went to another stall. In this stall there was toilet paper, and there was something else. There was a small amount of excrement smeared on the wall, and next to it, in black Sharpie pen, someone had scrawled, "This school is bullshit!"

I laughed out loud. Even at this fancy photo shoot, we could not escape the angry, immature graffiti of a mad little kid smearing shit on the wall. I loved this tiny, disgusting rebellion. I don't know why, but it made me feel better. "This photo shoot is bullshit," I thought, and went back to the room of gowns.

They were steaming the navy gown in anticipation of my arrival. I walked past the stylist and over to the other gowns. I picked my favorite one, an ornate dusty rose pink gown with a lace train.

ME: This is the one I'm going to wear.

STYLIST GUY (gently, as if to a fragile idiot): Zees will not fit you.

ME: Oh man, then we'd better get the seamstress to make this one fit, huh? We don't have too much time!

STYLIST GUY: She is only here for zee small alterations, not zee large-scale reworking of zee gown.

That's when I decided to just pretend as though I somehow had the power (in this weird situation, where no one was boss) to end arguments and make decisions.

ME: Well, I don't know what to say, because I just don't think I'd feel comfortable in anything but that.

When I played the "I don't feel comfortable" card, he knew it was over. "I don't feel comfortable" is the classic manipulative girl get-my-way line. It's right up there with "I don't feel entirely safe." Was it fair? Nope. Was it cool? Absolutely not. But it also wasn't fair or cool for him to have brought three dozen size-zero gowns to my photo shoot.

In the end, the seamstress literally cut open the back of one of the gowns and quickly added about a foot of canvas material to the back, pinned it together, and put it on me. The stylist was near tears at the destruction of the gown, but it fit like a glove—er, a glove that is kind of ugly and makeshift on the back. But on the front? Perfection. I love you, canvas. I love you, safety pins. If I ever do a voice in a Disney movie where I'm the princess whose friends are a bunch of inanimate household objects who come to life, I hope mine are a swatch of canvas and some sassy safety pins.

Later, in our gowns, I took Ellie to the bathroom and showed her the shit-stained graffiti. Ellie loved it, as I knew she would. I spent the rest of the shoot having a blast and posing goofily for photos with my pal, like the awesome, Most Beautiful, and Least Dressable, Girl that I was.

These Are the Narcissistic Photos
in My BlackBerry

I WOULD RATHER have someone read my diary than look at my iPod playlists. It's not because I have embarrassing playlists called "Setting the Mood for Sex-Time" or whatever. My playlists are humiliating because my workout mixes have dorky titles, like "Go for It, Girl!" and "You Can Do It, Mindy!" You might also see that some of my playlists are simply two songs on repeat fifteen times, like I'm a psycho getting pumped up to murder the president.

My BlackBerry photos, on the other hand, make me laugh. They are all horribly, horribly narcissistic. My BlackBerry camera has proven to exist primarily as a mirror to see if my makeup came out okay. The other ones are my favorite people who I want to look at all the time. I thought I'd share them all, uncensored.

1. I was on my way to a taping of *The Late Late Show with Craig Ferguson* and I wanted to see if the zit I had on the center of my forehead had shrunk. This is a different zit than the one I had when I was twenty-two, which was in the same spot and which I wrote about earlier in this book, but perhaps it was a descendant of that zit? It was so huge that Rainn Wilson advised me not to do the talk show appearance. I really wanted to go on *The Late Late*

Show, though, because I love Craig Ferguson, so I popped it with a safety pin sterilized with hot water in the women's restroom. A blood blob formed and dried up, and I was able to flick the crust off for the show, but you can still kind of see it.

2. I was on my way to the GQ Man of the Year Party. There was absolutely no reason for me to be there, but I'd heard Drake might perform. I did my own hair and I wanted to see if it looked awful.

3. I also wanted to see if my dress was too low-cut. I ultimately decided it was not too low-cut, but while wearing it, I had to keep my hands hovering over my cleavage, as though I were constantly overheated, like an old-timey Southern woman from a cartoon.

4. Yes, I am with my two best friends Brenda and Jocelyn who are very dear to me, blah blah, but this photo is more significant because it is a rare time where my head looks normal size. I have an *enormous* head, so it is important to me to have a few flattering, head-minimizing photos, in case I ever need to use them for one of those birthday cakes that have photographic icing.

5. I wasn't positive I could pull off big, black plastic glasses, so I took this photo. If you ever need to be a well-read, artsy hipster in a hurry you should really have big black plastic-framed glasses.

6. Now I needed to make sure I could pull off the glasses when I wasn't smiling. I look so f'ing cool here. I'm basically Claire Danes.

7. My boyfriend, David, doesn't end conversations with me by saying good-bye. He says, "LTFT" or "Last Thing, First Thing," which means I am the last thing he thinks about before bed and the first when he wakes up. Anyway, this awesome guy asked me to go see a Harry Potter movie. This is how he asked me, by sending me a photo of himself holding the ticket printouts. I love this photo.

8. I took my friend Sophia as my date to the Writers Guild Awards four years ago, and she was a perfect date. My dress is so weird, I look like I'm a real estate agent at a bachelorette party. Gross. I was also in a bad mood because I had just broken up with my boyfriend (not David, some old, forgettable boyfriend). I wasn't going to go at all, but Sophia made me and we had a great time.

9. I was thrilled about my pink checkerboard toenails. A whimsical toenail polish is one of the only places I believe whimsy should be allowed.

10. Ellie Kemper and I from shooting *The Office* episode "Classy Christmas," which I wrote. Ellie is wonderful because she never balks when I want to take pictures of us. I'm cheesy, and she celebrates it. I think I did a really good job of hiding the fact that I took the photo, making it look like some dude just randomly took a photo of two smiley, pretty girls, right?

11. I did my own eye makeup one night and was very excited about it. I took an extreme close-up in the hope that I would be able to follow what I did later on. It was not helpful. I also noticed some weird scar tissue on the whites of my eye, so I called my mom up in the middle of the night to ask her about it. It turned out to be nothing. I could delete this photo.

Revenge Fantasies While Jogging

IF IT WEREN'T FOR my imagination, I would weigh ten thousand pounds. This is because the only way I am able to exercise anymore is through a long and vivid revenge fantasy.

I'm not talking about revenge on real-life people I know, like, "Oh, Ed Helms cut in line at lunch, so I'm going to write that his character Andy gets super fat." That has some justice to it, since he seems to love food so much! I'm talking about elaborate *Kill Bill*–type stories, involving people who do not actually exist, where I play the lead role. Because revenge fantasies are such a big part of what I think about when I exercise, I've listed some of my greatest hits. Please integrate these into your own workouts, and say sayonara to calories!

MY HUSBAND IS MURDERED IN CENTRAL PARK ON AN IDYLLIC SPRING DAY

My husband was murdered by a serial killer in Central Park. We were walking by the reservoir one beautiful late-spring afternoon eating ice-cream cones and he was suddenly shot in the back of the head by a deranged man wearing an Antonin Scalia mask. "Scalia" runs away, cackling like the Joker, and hops into an Escalade and peels off. My handsome, innocent husband dies in my arms, the very night he was going to host *Saturday Night Live* for the first time. (Oh, yes, in this fantasy, my husband is a star point guard for the team that just won the NBA Finals.)

They get Jon Hamm to host a very somber *Saturday Night Live* that night. I can barely do the cameo I was going to do on Weekend Update. Yes, I still do the cameo. I'm sad, but come on—*SNL* cameo. Seth Meyers can't muster up the cheerfulness he usually has, either. The day's horrible events have marred everything.

After my husband's murder, I spend a lot of time doing push-ups and sit-ups, and I cut my hair very short while staring at myself in the mirror with dead eyes. I look like Mia Farrow at her height, but Indian and crazy toned. I stop enjoying my creature comforts, like junk food and hanging out with my friends, because nothing brings me pleasure but thoughts of revenge. My best friends give me the hurtful nickname "Count of Monte Cristo, But Boring," because I am bent on vengeance and it is getting tedious. However, because of my alienation and obsession, I am able to get in shape pretty fast, because all food tastes the same to me (like nothing), so I eat skinless chicken breasts and broccoli for every meal without complaint.

Scalia is in Miami. I find this out from a PI I hired who looks like Kris Kristofferson, but more grizzled. I go down there, hit the Kardashians' Dash boutique for a hot outfit, then infiltrate the South Beach club where I know Scalia hangs out. I am pretending to be a lesbian trainer. (Pretty easy to believe: my body is ripped and I have no interest in men anymore.) I find Scalia snorting coke in the back room, a lair of sorts. He has framed pictures of all the people he's murdered. I choke him to death with his own mask. When his body goes lifeless in my arms, I'm tempted to pull off the mask to see who it was. But I stop just before I do it. I don't even care anymore.

Total time taken up by this fantasy: 12 minutes
Total calories burned while having this fantasy: 90

THEY KIDNAP AND MURDER MY HUSBAND
ON OUR HONEYMOON

My new husband and I are vacationing in Buenos Aires. Some kind of terrorists who focus on interracial marriage (rare, I know, but terrible) want to make an example of me and my husband. They kidnap him and hold him for ransom, only to shoot him on live television the next day. At that moment, I stop speaking forever. I am a mute. But a mute who goes to the gym, for I run and do lunges and squats until I have no body fat anymore and can do fifty chin-ups and twenty-five pull-ups. Even in my revenge fantasy where all I do is exercise, I can still do only twenty-five pull-ups. Pull-ups are tough, no joke.

I race around Buenos Aires pretending to be a mute Indian tango dancer. But really, I'm trying to find the terrorists who killed my husband, which I do one late summer night. I stab them through the heart with a knife I keep hidden inside my massive hairdo.

When caught and put on trial in Argentina, I decide to represent myself. In my closing argument, I say, "In the country that saw so many disappearances in the 1970s, I'm surprised anyone cares about some terrorists disappearing from existence in the present day." Then, I disappear.

Total time taken up by this fantasy: 8 minutes
Total calories burned while having this fantasy: 65

I GET THAT WOMAN WHO WAS RUDE TO ME
AT SAKS IN TROUBLE

I'm in the Saks Fifth Avenue shoe department. I keep trying to get the attention of a snooty old-school Saks saleslady to try on a pair of Miu Miu pumps. I make the classic mistake of wearing my gym clothes to Saks, so she doesn't pay any attention to me. I finally approach her and flat-out ask for help, and she says she'll be right back. I sit down and wait for almost ten minutes and then find out she's helping a rich-looking white woman who is better dressed than me around the corner in the Louboutin section. I am so pissed I go to Customer Service, on the third floor, and fill out a complaint card against this woman.

Total time taken up by this fantasy: 1 minute
Total calories burned while having this fantasy: 10

AL QAEDA TAKES NBC'S *THE VOICE* HOSTAGE

On a big sweeps episode of NBC's *The Voice,* Al Qaeda drops from the ceiling on ropes and tries to turn it into a live terrorist competition where they kill innocent people every hour. The really sick part is they make the judges rate each murder. It's unbelievably shocking and horrible. Little did Al Qaeda know that I was sitting in the second row, having been given VIP tickets by my close, personal friend Adam Levine. I have a gun with me in my Alexander McQueen clutch—it's a plastic one that got by the metal detectors like John Malkovich had in *In the Line of Fire.* I wasn't sure why I packed my gun with me when I was getting ready to go to this taping of *The Voice,* but now I know.

When Al Qaeda gets ready to shoot their first victim on live TV, we hear a shot ring out! People scream. But no, it's not the innocent person they were about to shoot; it's the terrorist holding the innocent person. (I've seen this move in movies—the confusing "shot rang out" move. It is awesome.) The terrorists scramble. Who is this invisible antiterrorist? It's me, Mindy Kaling. I was hiding behind Cee Lo's fur coat, and no one saw me. Slowly, over the course of the night, I assassinate every terrorist with my sniper shooting. I train a group of plucky Girl

Scouts who are there on a field trip to be a distraction. Soon, the terrorists themselves are filled with terror. Pretty ironical, actually. And then, with the last one gunned down, the SWAT team pours in. I reveal myself and announce, "Song shall never be silenced by terror, only by being voted off." They continue the taping of *The Voice,* because otherwise, the terrorists would not have won exactly, but would have disrupted our evening of fun song judging.

Total time taken up by this fantasy: 20 minutes
Total calories burned: 200

My All-Important Legacy

Strict Instructions for My Funeral

WHOEVER IS closest to me when I die, here are the in-structions for my funeral. You might think this is pre-sumptuous, but consider it a favor to you, because at the time of my death, you will be so distracted with grief that your ability to plan will be compromised, and I don't want my funeral to be a thrown-together disaster.*

Dress code: chic devastated.

None of my exes are allowed to attend. Distracting. Weird. (Okay, the only way I would even consider an ex attending is if he were completely, horrifically devastated. Like, when he heard I died, it made him take a good hard look at his life and his choices, and he turned Buddhist or something.)

No current wives or girlfriends of my exes are allowed to at-tend. This part is really, for real, non-negotiable. They'll just use the opportunity to look all hot in black.

---

* *Thrown-Together Disaster Funeral* is my new HGTV show. It's a make-over funeral show where three flamboyant gay guys and a judgmen-tal sassy broad (think Wanda Sykes) crash a tacky funeral and fix it. Wanda's catchphrase is "Nuh-huh. Everyone out of this church. This funeral is a *disaster.*"

No one can use my funeral as the inciting incident for their own romantic comedy.

My a cappella group from college will try to perform. I forgive them for trying, but this is not allowed to happen. I don't just mean the group currently singing at my college. No assembly of past members or anything is allowed to sing. You must be vigilant about this. With a blink of an eye, I can see a group of tearful women starting a caterwauling rendition of Sarah McLachlan's "I Will Remember You." Be really mindful of this; they will find loopholes.

No one may use this occasion to debut original music they wrote. I hate original music.

There should be food at my funeral. I hate getting invited to something and there's no food. Something tasteful and light. No pasta. I'm serious. I will climb out of my coffin if anyone brings a baked ziti. Actually, no hot food at all. Small savory finger sandwiches, scones, coffee. Basically an English tea, but I don't want anything stacked on a tiered platter. That's pretentious.

People can text, but no phone calls. That's rude. And when I say you can text, I mean, hard-core furtive texting, like using one hand and with your BlackBerry hidden in your purse.

If people speak, they need to follow guidelines or this will become a free-for-all. I have a lot of comedy writer friends. Don't let them turn this into a roast for me. You know how I feel about roasts. I want no moments of mirth at all at this thing. No edgily remembering something stupid I did to show that we can all have a big, cathartic laugh.

Actually, no catharsis.

No irony at all. I mean it. I spent my entire professional career dealing in irony. I want an almost cringe-inducingly earnest ceremony.

Please, no religious stuff. I kind of insist no one mention

God or anything at my funeral. I'm not making some big atheist statement, but I want this to be solemn because people are so upset I'm dead, and I don't want to share the spotlight with God.

No candles. I hate candles. This isn't a sex scene from *Grey's Anatomy*.

If Steve Carell doesn't show up, I want my children and my children's children to make note of it.

There should be a gift bag for people when they leave. Inside of it should include: (1) a photo of me when I was my most beautiful, put through an old-timey photo process and displayed in a heart-shaped pewter frame. It should look like the kind of photo a soldier carried around with him during the Civil War; (2) an energy bar or a trendy body spray from whichever company is sponsoring the funeral; (3) a copy of a drawing I did when I was little of what I wanted to be when I grew up, which was an astronaut. Under the drawing should be written, in cursive, "She finally found her wings" or " . . . and we have lift-off"; and (4) a letter from the president talking about my impact on the creative community. If the president happens to be a woman that year, she can slant things that way, how I inspired her to believe in her own dreams and stuff.

Do all of this and you will know that I will rest in eternal peace. If that's important to you.

A Eulogy for Mindy Kaling,
by Michael Schur

My friend, former Office *writer and now creator of* Parks and Recreation,
Mike Schur supplied me with a eulogy in advance of my death.

F RIENDS, MEMBERS of Mindy's Family, Representatives of
Major Department Stores, good afternoon.

My name is Michael Schur, and I worked with Mindy Kaling
for several years on the TV program *The Office.* The American
version—not the Chinese version that has been running for the
past forty-one years.

Mindy's sudden death last week shocked me, as I'm sure it
also shocked the four women she was fighting over those shoes
with during the Dubai Bloomingdale's Midnight Madness Sale.
Though the stabbing has been labeled "accidental," those of
us who knew Mindy knew it was only a matter of time before a
luxury-goods-based brawl would do her in. And if there's a silver
lining to all of this, it's that I had "Impaled by Heel of Christian
Louboutin Jem Suede Peep-Toe Slingback" in the "How Will
Mindy Kaling Die?" pool that Rainn Wilson has been running
since 2006, so I won $200.

I'll never forget the Mindy Kaling that I met on our first
day of work: bright-eyed, green, a complete novice in the world

of television writing . . . and yet somehow far more confident than everyone else. She was *supremely* confident. Braggy, maybe. Cocky? What's the right word . . . let's go with talggy, which is a word I just made up that means "talkative and braggy."

Her work ethic was second to none. And by that I mean: if you made a list of all the levels of work ethics, hers would be just above "none." One day she came into work so late it was the next morning. And for that morning, she was also late. And hungover. But we forgave her, because when we tried to bring it up, she just started talking about how hot some actor was, and then how much she loved Italian ice, and then how Beyoncé should release a country album, and then a bunch of other stuff, and we got tired and just forgot about the whole thing.

Mindy wore a lot of hats. Ivy League graduate, actor, comedian, playwright, inveterate gossip, weirdly pro-gun Republican, outspoken advocate of conspicuous consumption, and of course—as we learned upon the posthumous release of her puffy-sticker-covered diaries—hard-core perv. But despite all of these foibles and flaws, and the literally thousands of others I jotted down in my psychotherapist-mandated "Mindy Workbook"

This is Mike and me at the Writers Guild of America annual awards.
We lost every category and got drunk in the hotel lobby.

in order to maintain a sense of professionalism while we worked together, I loved Mindy Kaling. No one wrote like Mindy. No one was funnier than Mindy. No one else, in short, *was* Mindy. This will not be true for long, I understand, as her will dictates that her DNA be replicated one million times, news that recently sent the NYSE Retail Shopping Index skyrocketing.

I can't believe she's gone. I console myself by thinking, *Well, I guess the angels just wanted her to shut up.* I will miss her dearly, and I hope that she is up in heaven right now watching us and smiling, even though deep down I know that if there is an afterlife, she's a pretty much open-and-shut case for hell.

R.I.P.

Good-bye

WHEN I WAS six and I saw *The Sound of Music* for the first time, my favorite part, hands down, was when the Von Trapp children bid farewell to partygoers with their song "So Long, Farewell" from the stairway of their Austrian manor. As an adult, I now see what a terrible example this is for children. It teaches them that adults will be charmed by long, protracted musical good-byes. In fact, all of *The Sound of Music* inspired a childhood's worth of my misguided behavior, where I believed people would always be excited to hear me sing.

I memorized the song off our record player. Then, at bedtime, I called my parents to the landing of the stairs in our house so that I could perform it in its entirety. Just me singing all seven kids' parts, accompanied by no music. Once I finished one child's part, I disappeared into my bedroom only to reemerge and run down the stairs to pick up the next one's part. My parents listened patiently until we got to the second kid's exit.

"Okay, enough of this," my dad said, and headed up the stairs to shuffle me off to bed.

"We're only on Friedrich! There are five more Von Trapp children!" I said. This fell on deaf ears. My parents were supportive of my creativity but did not have a lot of patience for whimsy with zero production value. They had stuff to do.

The point is I learned nothing from this experience. Yes, if I'm at a party where I'm not enjoying myself, I will put some cookies in my jacket pocket and leave without saying good-bye. But when I'm having a great time? I like 'em nice and drawn out, Von Trapp–style. I could say good-bye all day. Like a guy putting on his shoes.

Before I leave, I thought I'd answer any remaining questions you might have.

So, you never won any childhood spelling bees? I was under the impression this was a memoir of a spelling bee champ.
It is confusing, I know. Based on my ethnicity, the number of friends I had as a kid, my build, my eyesight, and my desire to please my parents, I should have been the reigning spelling bee champion from ages seven to fourteen. My best guess at an explanation is that my parents were worried I would be just too good a speller and a potential kidnap prospect for anyone watching the Scripps National Spelling Bee on CSPAN-3 in the middle of the afternoon.

Why didn't you talk about whether women are funny or not?
I just felt that by commenting on that in any real way, it would be tacit approval of it as a legitimate debate, which it isn't. It would be the same as addressing the issue of "Should dogs and cats be able to care for our children? They're in the house anyway." I try not to make it a habit to seriously discuss nonsensical hot-button issues.

What will your next book be about?
I hope my next book will be about my husband, my kids, my cool movie career, and sharing all the things I learned about

since I wrote this book. Like, I'd love to know where my natural lip line is. I still have no clue. Maybe by then I'll have figured that out.

Anything else?
Not really. I just, I don't want to say good-bye.

See you guys soon.

Love,
Mindy

Acknowledgments

I'D LIKE TO THANK my sweet and funny friends who helped me with this. They are: Jeremy Bronson, Danny Chun, Alexis Deane, Lena Dunham, Brent Forrester, Dan Goor, Charlie Grandy, Steve Hely, Carrie Kemper, Ellie Kemper, Paul Lieberstein, Danielle Moffett, Sophia Rossi, Deb Schoeneman, Mike Schur, and Deborah Tarica. Quick-witted Ava Tramer was an all-star of organization with the demeanor of a doe. B. J. Novak was a terrific friend and editor, giving me sound notes like "Hey, Mindy, I think you sound kind of racist here. I would be really careful about not sounding racist in your book." Greg Daniels has been key to just about everything I've done these past eight years. He's the best.

Thanks to my dearest: Christina Hoe, Jocelyn Leavitt, Brenda Withers, David Harris, and my brother, Vijay, for letting me tell stories and share photos of them, which I suppose they kind of had to do out of love, anyway.

I am grateful to Maya Mavjee, Tina Constable, Tammy Blake, Meredith McGinnis, and Anna Thompson for their support, hard work, and excitement about this book.

Melissa Stone and Alex Crotin were sweethearts and bad-asses, which is very difficult to pull off.

Without Howard Klein I would never have written this. Richard Abate guided me through this entire process with patience and love. I have both of their cell phone numbers, a privilege which I abuse.

I love NBC, even though I have never gotten a GE discount.

Suzanne O'Neill is a brilliant editor with whom I've had almost daily contact. Long ago, I blurred the line of professionalism with her, and there is no going back. She is my friend. Sorry, Suzanne.

And finally, I want to thank Avu and Swati Chokalingam. I know I dedicated this book to them, but I guess I'm just one of those weird kids who likes their parents too much.